THE BRANDENBURG QUEST

A TRUE STORY

Based on the book

QUEST

by

Ib Melchior with Frank Brandenburg

Screenplay by Ib Melchior

The story of QUEST is true. The central figure, Frank Brandenburg, today lives in Hildesheim, Germany.

SIMON WIESENTHAL

Allow me to call your attention to a property which I strongly feel would make an outstanding motion picture. It is a book by Ib Melchior, the author and motion picture director, and my friend, Frank Brandenburg, whose exciting and amazing story is told in the book. I personally know Mr. Brandenburg and can vouch for the veracity of the events described in the book, even though they may seem almost unbelievable. Mr. Brandenburg sent several years infiltrating the still existing Nazi conspiracy and his exploits in many instances re-write history.

I know you are always looking for properties that are exciting, inspiring and if possible true. Mr. Brandenburg's "QUEST" is all of this and much more.

I would deem it a personal favor if you would consider reading it. Frank Brandenburg's story would become a high ranking and top class movie.

With my best personal regards, I am.

Simon Wiesenthal

THE BRANDENBURG QUEST
A TRUE STORY

THE UNPRODUCED SCREENPLAY

IB MELCHIOR

The Brandenburg Quest: A True Story
© 2015 Ib Melchior. All Rights Reserved.

No part of this book may be reproduced in any form or by any means, electronic, mechanical, digital, photocopying or recording, except for the inclusion in a review, without permission in writing from the publisher.

Published in the USA by:
BearManor Media
PO Box 71426
Albany, GA 31708
www.bearmanormedia.com

ISBN 978-1-59393-856-7

Library of Congress Control Number: 2015914480
BearManor Media, Albany, GA

Printed in the United States of America.
Book design by John Teehan

FADE IN

1   EXT. STOIZENDORF, AUSTRIA—MOUNTAIN ROAD—DAY

A CAR is driving up the road. The driver is FRANK BRANDENBURG, twenty, blue-eyed with a shock of blonde hair.

2   EXT. APPROACH TO FRANZ LECHNER'S FARM COMPOUND—DAY

The compound is surrounded by a fence. A heavy gate stands open. Frank turns into the farmyard. A farmhouse stands beyond the yard.

3   EXT. FRANZ LECHNER'S COMPOUND—DAY

Frank drives up and parks his car. As soon as he starts to step out, TWO BIG BLACK DOGS come charging out from behind a woodpile in SNARLING fury.

Heart-pounding, he jumps back in the car and slams the door, watching, breathless, as the dogs claw and scratch at the car door.

Over and over again, the frenzied beasts hurl themselves in rage at the car, the furious barking obliterating all other sounds.

Frank's shaking hand touches the gear shift…then slowly he removes it. He's come too far to go back now.

He leans on the horn. At the sound, the dogs double their efforts to get at him. He keeps honking the horn, watching the door to the house. Finally it opens and a man steps through into the yard. FRANZ LECHNER, unkempt dirty-blond hair, clad in dark, soiled trousers held up by grey suspenders, a light blue shirt, open at the neck, partly buttoned and so carelessly tucked in that a flash of pale skin shows above his fly. He walks up to the car.

>   LECHNER
>   (to the dogs)
> *Ruhe!*

At once the dogs fall silent.

>   LECHNER
> *Zu fuss!*

The dogs immediately take up their positions flanking Lechner.

>   LECHNER
> *Aufpassen!*

The dogs fix their eyes on Frank, snarling menacingly. Lechner turns to Frank.

> LECHNER
>
> What do you want?

> FRANK
>
> Are—are you Herr Franz Lechner?

Lechner glares at him.

> LECHNER
>
> Get out!

Fearful of the dogs, Frank complies.

> LECHNER
>
> Come!

He turns on his heels and followed by the ever watchful dogs—and Frank—he walks toward the heavy gate to his farmyard.

THE MAIN TITLES OVER THE FOLLOWING

Lechner slams the gate shut and bars it. Frank looks around, a prisoner now. The cobblestone yard is unkempt, in need of repair: broken farm equipment, debris and trash lie strewn in piles; a few scraggly HENS peck listlessly at the remains of a dungheap.

To the right, a farmhouse of square stone blocks is heavily festooned with row upon row of dried corncobs through which grimy, multi-paned windows look out. A broom lies unused on the ground next to the door.

Frank and Lechner—followed by the dogs—walk to the house. Lechner gestures at the door.

END OF MAIN TITLES

> LECHNER
>
> Inside.

4   INT. LECHNER'S HOUSE—DAY

Lechner gestures Frank across the room. He motions to a straight-backed chair at a large table.

> LECHNER
>
> Sit.

Lechner sits down opposite Frank. He opens a drawer. He pulls out a snub-nosed gun. Ceremoniously he places it on the table.

LECHNER
Now we shall find out who you are. What do you want?

He puts his hand on the gun. CAMERA ZOOMS in to a CLOSE SHOT of the gun.

5   EXT. YARD—DAY

6   CU of a Luger gun. It is held in the hand of a man. It fires.

7   WIDER ANGLE

We see a man—now dead, having been shot in the back of the head by a man in the Nazi SS uniform—tumble down into a deep hole heaped with other dead bodies. CAMERA PULLS BACK to reveal that the image is on a B&W TV set. We are in—

8   INT. FRANK BANDENBURG'S ROOM—EVENING

We are watching a film—*THE HOLOCAUST*—on a thirteen-inch BLACK-AND-WHITE TV. The CAMERA continues to PULL BACK to reveal:

FRANK BRANDENBURG, just turned 16, sits cross-legged on a bed in his garret bedroom, eyes wide, glued to the screen.

Blue eyes in an impish face look out from a lock of hair that falls, untamed, across his brow; he has the slight, gangly look of a typical teen.

A small Dachshund, GRITTI, lies curled up in his lap.

(NOTE: At the director's discretion, Gritti may be present in the scenes where Frank is at home)

SUPER: HILDESHEIM, WEST GERMANY (1979)

An angry and stunned FRANK watches the IMAGES OF THE HOLOCAUST in the FILM, as he strokes Gritti.

9   CLOSE SHOT—TV SCREEN

A particularly horrifying scene unfolds on the screen.

10   WIDER ANGLE

Suddenly Frank gets up. With a yelp Gritti tumbles from his lap. Angrily Frank strides to the TV set and abruptly turns it off. For a moment he stands staring at the dead set, obviously grievously disturbed.

FRANK
How dare they? How DARE they!!?

11   EXT. BRANDENBURG NURSERY—NEXT DAY

Frank makes his way though rows of SAPLINGS. In the distance, marking the boundary of the family nursery and its seven greenhouses, the GRAVESTONES of a well tended cemetery stand in sharp contrast to the cheerful green surroundings of the family's large, two-story white house.

Frank's father, KARL-PETER, potting a sapling, reproaches his son without looking up.

KARL-PETER
Up late again, Frank? We're going to have to take it take away. You have homework…and where have you been? You were supposed to have helped your mother at the flower stand. Do you think you can act like an American now, because you have your own TV?

FRANK
Papa, I saw this American movie last night. It was called—the—the Holocaust. It was awful.

KARL-PETER
I have heard they made such a film.

FRANK
But, Papa, it—it was full of terrible lies. About the German people. It—it couldn't be true, could it? Was it, Papa?

KARL-PETER
I was young, Frank. Just a child. Your mother was three years old when the war ended. We were too young to remember much.

FRANK
But Opa, and Oma. What do they know?

KARL-PETER
Your grandfather doesn't like to talk about it.

12   EXT. HILDESHEIM OPEN MARKET—FLOWER STAND—SAME DAY

Frank and his mother, ILSE, a strikingly pretty woman, stand behind banks of flowers. Frank wraps a bouquet of anemones with red ribbon and hands it to an OLDER WOMAN.

OLDER WOMAN
Dankeschön.

She leaves. Frank glances quickly at his mother, arranging flowers with more attention than usual.

                FRANK

But why not here?

                ILSE

Hush, we have customers. Here—
        (hands him the flowers)
—use blue ribbon on this one.

                FRANK

But did it happen, Mama? Like it says in the movie?

                ILSE

Movies are movies, *bübschen*. It was a long time ago.
        (beat)
And don't ask grandpa or grandma. It will only upset them.

13   INT. NURSERY OFFICE

Frank stands before his father's SECRETARY, 62, certain he's found someone old enough to remember. His arms are crossed and he leans back, triumphant, waiting. Instead, she throws her hands up in dismay.

                SECRETARY

Junge! Junge! You are treading on forbidden ground. It could be a dangerous thing to pursue. No one today wants to talk about all that. Let it be.

14   EXT. CHURCH—DAY

LONG SHOT

15   INT. CHURCH—DAY

TWO SHOT, FRANK and PASTOR

The Pastor pats Frank's shoulder patronizingly.

                PASTOR

Let it be, Frank. It was a long time ago. Why rake up old times? Let it be.

FRANK looks disappointed, concerned.

| 16 | EXT. HIGH SCHOOL—DAY |

INT. CLASS ROOM—DAY

| 17 | TWO SHOT FRANK AND TEACHER |

> TEACHER
> It was a long time ago, Frank. Yes—we did have some—some trouble with the Jews. But it is over now. It is nothing you should concern yourself about. Why wake a sleeping dog? You have your studies to do, *that* is important…

FRANK looks disappointed but stubborn.

| 18 | INT. HILDESHEIM—BOOKSTORE—DAY |

Frank searches the book shelves, running his hands over the spines. He pulls one out, sets it aside, then continues.

Curious, the BOOKSELLER comes over and picks up one of the books.

> BOOKSELLER
> Interesting…
> (sizes him up)
> Not exactly what you'd find at your standard gymnasium library, *ja*?
> (beat)
> Is there anything I can help you with?

Frank shakes his head, mystified.

> FRANK
> I'm looking for *Mein Kampf*. It isn't anywhere.

The Bookseller stiffens, then glances around nervously to make certain no one is there to overhear.

> BOOKSELLER
> (low)
> It isn't sold in Germany.
> (off Frank's quizzical look)
> It's not allowed.

Frank scowls.

                           BOOKSELLER
                        (motions him forward)
    Come with me.

Frank follows him—

INTO A BACK ROOM—THROUGH A DOOR—DOWN A NARROW STAIRWAY

19   INT. BASEMENT—CONTINUOUS

The Bookseller turns on a bare overhead bulb. The dust is thick everywhere. He crosses to shelves and pulls down a book, blows the dust off, then hands it to Frank.

                           BOOKSELLER
    Voila! You know "voila," yes?
                            (chuckles)

Frank opens to the title page, then looks up, wide-eyed. The Bookseller is already starting up the stairs.

                           BOOKSELLER
    Three marks.

He stops, turns back to Frank and gives him a conspiratorial nod.

                           BOOKSELLER
    You didn't get it here.

20   INT. BRANDENBURG HOUSE—BEDROOM—NIGHT

Frank sits reading on his bed surrounded by books and with Gritti in his lap. The door opens and his grandfather comes into the room. Frank looks up but says nothing as the old man picks up a couple of the books and reads the titles aloud.

                            WILHELM
    "The Auschwitz Lie." "Inside the Third Reich."

                             FRANK
    It's very confusing, Opa. Some say the Americans built the
    ovens to make it look like we did; they say the concentration
    camps were built as movie sets; they say it's all…Hollywood.
    But some—

                            WILHELM
                       (finishing his sentence)
    Some say it was real.
                          (he sits down)

I was in the NSKK: Basically we were engaged in traffic control. Yes—we wore brown shirts with Swastikas; we had to, to keep our jobs, but we were not—Nazis. Back then—we thought we were building a new Germany, a beautiful future.
>(he sighs)

We know some of what happened…and some we will never know.

FRANK

But if it happened, why don't they teach it in school? And if it didn't, why did Hollywood make it up?
>(grabs a book)

And what about Bormann? The "Grey Emminence". The most powerful man in Germany—after Hitler. What about him?
>(he gestures at his books)

They have a lot to say about him.

WILHELM

I am sure they do.

FRANK

Some say he was killed. In Berlin. Others say they saw him, *after* the war. Who's right? How can such a prominent man simply disappear? It smells, Opa. It smells.
>(pause)

Did you know him?

WILHELM

I told you, I wasn't one of them. They were powerful men. Very powerful. We only followed their orders. We were afraid of them.

FRANK
>(grabs another book)

It says *here* he's still alive.

WILHELM

Why do you care? Bormann is dead. And buried like the past should be.
>(motions to TV)

What happened to your television? You've lost interest?
>(shakes his head)

You young people today. You have to have something, then, as soon as you get it—
>(breaks off and rises to go)

In my day…

                    (drops what he was going to say)
> It's late. Go to sleep. And let the past do the same. Goodnight.

He leaves. FRANK picks up a book and starts reading.

DISSOLVE TO:

21   INT. BRANDENBURG HOUSE—BEDROOM—NIGHT

Frank's room is cluttered with books—books open on the bed and stacked about the room in three- and four-foot piles. A RED POSTER with a BLACK SWASTIKA is taped over his desk.

SUPER: HILDESHEIM, TWO YEARS LATER

Frank, now 18, is stuffing items into a duffel bag on the bed. Satisfied, he stops and checks himself in the mirror, slicks back his hair and studies a pimple forming on his face.

                    ILSE (O.S.)
> Frank! Dinner!

22   INT. BRANDENBURG HOUSE—KITCHEN—NIGHT

Frank enters, duffel bag in hand, to find his family seated at the table waiting for him; Ilse, Karl-Peter, Wilhelm and his younger sister, ULRIKE. All eyes go to his duffel bag.

                    KARL-PETER
> And where do you think you're going at this hour?

                    FRANK
> I am taking the night train to Munich—for my research.

                    KARL-PETER
> For God's sake, Frank, why?

                    ILSE
> Sit and eat.

                    FRANK
> They call it the "cradle of Nazism." I have to—

                    ILSE
                    (over)
> You can't—

                    FRANK
                    (over)
    I'm eighteen now. I can do what I—

                    KARL-PETER
                    (cutting him off)
    You can't just do what you want.

                    FRANK
    No, but I can do what I have to do. And I have to see it for
    myself.
                    (starts out)
    I'll call you from Munich.

    Karl-Peter puts a restraining hand on Ilse's arm and signals
    for her to let him go. Ulrike jumps up and grabs him, giving
    him a good-bye hug.

                    ULRIKE
    Be careful, Frank.
                    (smiles up at him)
    And I think you've very brave.

                                                    DISSOLVE TO:

23 CLOSE ON—*DER GLOCKENSPIEL*

    The mechanical GOLDEN ROOSTER of the famous clock at the top of the New Town Hall,
    CROWS to announce the coming hour.

    Trumpeters appear; then Standard-Bearers herald the noble Knights. The first appears,
    charges and misses; the second charges, unhorsing the RED KNIGHT. Red-Coated FOLK
    DANCERS emerge, dancing, followed by a QUEEN who comes out and gives her blessing.

    At last the Golden Rooster returns, one last time, to signal the end, then disappears into the
    mechanical world of make-believe time and its intricate pageantry.

    Forty-three BELLS ring out in majesty.

    The CAMERA PANS DOWN.

24 EXT. MUNICH—MARIENPLAZ—DAY

    Frank—like any tourist—stands among a GROUP OF TOURISTS staring up at the clock.

    The crowd disperses and he takes out a note pad, checks an address, checks his own watch,
    and heads out.

EXT. MUNICH—PRINZREGENTENSTRASSE—DAY

Frank stands staring at the apartment building where Hitler had his private apartment in the early days. He takes a snapshot—also like a tourist—and makes a few notes in his note pad.

> FRANK (V.O.)
> The Führer's apartment. Early days. Number eighteen Prinz-regentenstrasse.

25 EXT. MUNICH—OSTERIA BAVARIA RESTAURANT—DAY

Frank stands across the street looking at the restaurant.

Frank raises his camera and takes several wide shots…then crosses the street and enters the restaurant.

INT. OSTERIA BAVARIA RESTAURANT—CONTINUOUS

Frank whispers to the Maitre'd who motions to an old man, the OWNER, to come over. The Owner listens intently to what Frank has to say, then beams.

> OWNER
> They very table! Follow me.

MOMENTS LATER.

Frank sits at a table by the window, looking around, pleased with himself.

DISSOLVE TO:

The owner comes over and leans down to advise Frank on his order.

> OWNER
> He liked the eggplant…but spaghetti was a great favorite too.

Frank turns the cutlery over, fork in one hand, knife in the other.

> OWNER
> Ah, yes, HE could have used that very same fork and knife.
> Nothing has changed much—since then.

We see a CLOSE SHOT of the knife. It has a sharp point and an intricately and identifiably carved handle.

> FRANK
> Spaghetti, please, and…

The Brandenburg Quest

>   (re fork and spoon)
>   …can I buy these?

>   OWNER
>   (shaking his head, no)
>   You may *have* them. For your 'quest,' my boy.
>   (chuckles)
>   Now all you need is the Holy Grail to go along with them, no?

DISSOLVE TO:

26   INT/EXT. TRAM (MOVING)—NEXT DAY

Frank takes the tram from Munich to Geiselgasteig.

27   EXT. GEISELGASTEIG—BAVARIAFILMPLAZ 7—STUDIO GATE—DAY

Frank stands looking up at the studio. He approaches, hopeful, and addresses the Security Guard. The Guard, barely glancing up, motions him on his way. Without a pass, it's impossible to get in. Hopes dashed, Frank turns away.

28   EXT. GEISELGASTEIG—TRAM STATION—PLATFORM—DAY

Frank waits for the next tram. It pulls up and he is about to get on when a GROUP of blond, blue-eyed boys about his age spill out and head—*en masse*—towards the studio.

As he watches them go, his face lights up and he hurries after them. Catching up, he attempts to blend in, laughing at the tail-end of jokes, elbow-to-elbow with strangers.

29   EXT. GEISELGASTEIG—BAVARIAFILMPLAZ 7—STUDIO GATE—DAY

Back at the gate, the guard looks at Frank, the boy seems vaguely familiar—but, then, they all look alike. He waves Frank through.

30   EXT. BAVARIA FILM—STUDIO LOT—DAY

Frank finds himself in a line trying to look as inconspicuous as possible. He gets to the front where a WOMAN in a ticket booth is focused on a clipboard.

>   WOMAN
>   Name, age, height, address?

>   FRANK
>   Brandenburg, Frank. Eighteen, five feet—

She stops him in mid-sentence.

                                WOMAN
           You're not on the list.

                                FRANK
           There must be a mistake. Please. Check it again. I've come a
           long way…

He babbles in generalities—with no idea of why he's there. She peers at him over her glasses, then scribbles his name on the bottom of the list…

                                WOMAN
           Two doors down, on your right. Next!

31   A SERIES OF SHOTS

Frank is transformed into a member of HITLER YOUTH.

(A)   Frank sits in a barber chair. In three minutes his hair is barely visible ending only with a tuft, like a rooster's comb, perched high on the top of his head. Next!

(B)   Inside a small room, a man hands him a bundle of clothes. Next! Frank looks down to see—

(C)   A BROWN SHIRT with RED ARMBAND on the left sleeve, WHITE BAND circling the red and a BLACK SWASTIKA on a square white field. Hitler Youth. Next!

(D)   Frank leans back in a chair before a large mirror while makeup is being applied. He is enjoying this immensely.

(E)   Frank and the other boys, now in costume, are herded onto a big bus. They are now movie extras!

(F)   The Group sits on a crowded bus as they are driven to the center of Munich—to the House of German Art. The excitement is high.

32   INT. HAUS DER DEUTSCHEN KUNST—MOVIE SET

The House of German Art is being used as the set for an ABC special, "Inside the Third Reich." Frank is talking to one of the look-alike boys with blond hair and finely chiseled features when he catches sight of the CREW off to one side.

An ASSISTANT leans against a wall, taking a break, smoking a cigarette before the chaos of the shoot. Frank wanders over to him. They take each other in.

                                ASSISTANT
           First time, eh *Junge*?

Frank nods yes, and looks around the set. In the center, a disheveled man is screaming at the top of his lungs.

                    FRANK
              (points to man)
Who is that shouting?

                    ASSISTANT
The director. Chomsky. American, of course.

                    FRANK
              (pointing again)
And who's that?

33   CLOSE ON—a MAN in full regalia of a NAZI Lieutenant General, leaning against a wall, sucking on a can of Coke.

BACK TO SCENE

                    ASSISTANT
Ah, he's supposed to be General Baur. Hans Baur. Hitler's personal pilot.
              (looks more closely)
He does look a little like Baur. Minus forty years, and the Coke, of course.
              (he chuckles)
Hollywood and Coke have brought many a good man down.

The joke flies over Frank's head as he turns the name "Baur" over in his mind.

                    ASSISTANT
He only limps in character.

                    FRANK
Limps?

                    ASSISTANT
Yes. The real Baur limps. Lost a leg in the war.

                    FRANK
How?

                    ASSISTANT
He was a prisoner of war. In Russia. He'd been wounded in the leg, and the wound became gangrenous. It had to come off.

FRANK is totally absorbed. Flattered the ASSISTANT continues.

				ASSISTANT (cont)
The Russians had no equipment. No scalpels. No surgical saws. Nothing. But they did take off the leg. At the knee.

				FRANK
But—how?

				ASSISTANT
They used someone's pen knife.

				FRANK
My God!

				ASSISTANT
But his limp is very slight. I hardly noticed it, when he was here.

				FRANK
Hans Baur? You've seen him? The real Hans Baur?

				ASSISTANT
Jawohl. Here. At the studio. Advising on the so-called technical details. Seemed like a nice enough guy. He's here in Munich—but he hasn't been around since then.

				FRANK
Munich!!! Here? In Munich? Hey—do I have a minute?

				ASSISTANT
You got about eighty hours at the rate these Americans work—
				(calling out to Frank as he rushes off)
—but don't go far.

34	EXT. MUNICH STREET—PHONE BOOTH—DAY

Frank is on the phone, the Munich phone directory open in the booth.

				FRANK
				(into phone)
By any chance do you know where I can reach him?

				WOMAN'S VOICE (V.O.)
				(over the phone)
We've had a few calls like this before. We do not know him. All I know is that he is supposed to live in Herrsching am Ammersee. Good-bye.

CLICK. An excited Frank calls information.

                        FRANK
Do you have a phone number for a Hans Baur in Herrsching am Ammersee?
                        (pause)
Yes, yes...

He writes a number hurriedly, then dials again.

                        VOICE (V.O.)
                        (over the phone)
Baur hier.

Frank's heart leaps.

35   INT/EXT—S-BAHN (RAPID TRANSIT)—DAY

Frank sits stiffly holding a large box of CHOCOLATES in his lap as the countryside flies by.

36   EXT. HERRISCHING AM AMMERSEE—NEUWIDDERSBERG—HOUSE—DAY

Frank stands before a white Bavarian villa, brown shutters, a fountain and tidy garden in the front yard.

Tightly clutching his chocolates, he knocks. The door opens. Frank is startled by what he sees:

HANS BAUR, 84, a short, slovenly man with a beer belly, wears a worn brown sweater over an open shirt and unpressed brown pants.

SUPER: HANS BAUR

                        FRANK
General—Baur?

                        BAUR
Herr Brandenburg, I presume. Come in, come in.

Frank takes a deep breath...and steps inside.

37   INT. BAUR'S VILLA—HALLWAY

A small DACHSHUND comes running, then stops to sniff Frank's shoes. A woman, FRAU BAUR, follows the Dachshund.

                        BAUR
My wife.

Frank bows politely and holds out the chocolates.

FRANK

Bitte, gnädige Frau.

She beams and takes them.

FRAU BAUR
Thank you, thank you, very much.
(to Hans)
You have such considerate friends, Hans.

BAUR
(motioning Frank forward)
Come, we shall go into the living room, yes?

He walks ahead with a decided limp.

38 INT. BAUR'S VILLA—LIVING ROOM

All is neat and unexceptional except for a BRONZE BUST OF HITLER and, on a table, framed PHOTOS of a much younger Baur with other Nazis: HESS, BORMANN, MUSSOLINI, HITLER…On the wall, an engraving of Hitler is prominently displayed.

All three sit. Frank looks at Baur and sees a gentle, kindly old man. Baur smiles.

BAUR
Now, young man, what do you want from me?

A man sticks his head in the door.

MAN
Sir. It is time.

BAUR
Sofort.
(he turns to Frank)
You must excuse me, Herr Brandenburg. I have a small duty to perform. Won't take long. Perhaps you would like to accompany me?

FRANK
I should be pleased.

They exit.

The Brandenburg Quest

39 INT. HEN-HOUSE ROOKERY—DAY

SHOT BAUR AND FRANK

They're standing at a table on which are two trays with newly hatched chicks and a pail. BAUR is taking a chick from one tray, examining it and placing it in the other tray. Behind him is a double row of single cages, each holding a hen; it has a small hole in front through which the hen can stick out its head.

> BAUR
> We raise our own layers. Nothing elaborate. Just enough for us and a few friends.

He motions toward the first tray of tiny little yellow chicks milling about.

> BAUR
> Each new batch of chicks must be inspected. Some are not perfect—like this one—

He holds out a chick for Frank to see.

40 CLOSE SHOT CHICK

It has an appendage which seems to be a third leg.

> BAUR
> They must, of course, be eliminated.

He tosses the chick toward the pail; he misses and the chick hits the rim, falls off and tumbles to the ground, just as the MAN wheels a cart past. One of the wheels crush the chick, as the cart moves on.

BAUR bends down and scoops up the remains in his hand. For a moment he contemplates it—then he holds it out to one of the hens behind him.

> BAUR
> (Obviously amused)
> Here, little mother. Put it back where it came from!

He cackles. The hen pecks at the chick remains.

41 CLOSE SHOT

The HEN is pecking at the pitiful remains in Bauer's hand.

42 INT. BAUR'S LIVING ROOM—DAY—CLOSE SHOT MRS. BAUR

She is sitting on the sofa; with relish she plops a piece of chocolate into her mouth.

43 WIDER ANGLE

>   FRANK and BAUR are sitting together.

>> BAUR
>> It was the Führer's most ardent wish. Keep the German people, the German race pure, he would say. Pure and non-contaminated. Perfect.

>> FRANK
>> I—I should like to know as much about the Führer as you can tell me. What was he like?

> A beat. BAUR sizes Frank up. The boy clearly isn't a spy. BAUR leans back, comfortably, reminiscing.

>> BAUR
>> *Unser Vati*—our Dad—was one of the greatest men the world will ever see. A true genius!

>> FRANK (O.C.)
>> (tentatively)
>> Herr Baur…some call him a monster.

> Baur chuckles good-humoredly, unfazed.

>> BAUR
>> There has been much falsehood written about *unser Vati* by people who have never met him, much less known him. But the Führer was truly a remarkable man, kind and considerate.

> Frank leans in, giving it all he's got.

>> FRANK
>> But—what about all the stories I've read? Concentration camps. The atrocities. Mass murderers, gassings. Millions killed, they say. They call it the "Holocaust."

> For a moment Baur studies him closely, then smiles.

>> BAUR
>> My dear boy, you *are* naïve.

>> FRANK
>> But I've seen pictures. And a film. I've read books about these places. Auschwitz. Bergen-Belsen. Books with terrible pictures of people. Jews. Starving…

                    BAUR
It's true many of the inmates were Jews…
                    (shrugs, indifferent)

                    FRAU BAUR
                    (breaking in, cheerful)
I think our young guest might like a cup of coffee. Don't you think so, Hans?
                    (smiling at Frank)
And some *Apfelstrudel*, yes? It's freshly made. I shall get it while you two go on with your nice little chat.

She leaves the room.

Baur leans forward in his chair and looks closely at Frank, fixing him with a stare.

                    BAUR
The Jew is a curious creature, my young friend. He either hogs everything for himself at the expense of others, or he wallows in self-pity and degradation—mental and physical.
                    (shrugs again)
The horror stories you have heard, about the camps are all lies. Lies made up by the enemies of Germany. Lies to discredit the Fatherland.

                    FRANK
But—the pictures. Of the—of the camps?

                    BAUR
Those camps you saw photos of, those 'showcase camps' one can still visit today, were all built by the Allies *after* the war. They are nothing but manufactured evidence against us.
                    (shakes his head sadly)
Your Holocaust, my dear boy, is a lie. It never happened.

Frau Baur returns with an ornately carved wooden tray.

                    FRAU BAUR
I think you will like the strudel, Herr Brandenburg, it is my own recipe.

She places cups, saucers and flowered plates on the table.

                    FRAU BAUR
A little extra of the really yummy stuff.

She plops a large piece of strudel on Frank's plate with a pair of silver tongs, then holds the tongs out to him.

                        FRAU BAUR

A gift. From the Herr Reichsminister Dr. Joseph Goebbels. He gave us such a lovely set of silverware. So sweet of him, *nicht wahr*?

Frank stares at the spoon he's stirring his coffee with—possibly Goebbels'—then looks up.

                              FRANK
                           (to Baur)

Sir, why do you think Dr. Goebbels and his wife decided to die in the Bunker and poisoned their children rather than escape?

                                BAUR

I would have stayed with *unser Vati* too—but he ordered me to stay with Reichsleiter Bormann. For as long as the Reichsleiter…needed me.

                              FRANK

For what? It was over.

                                BAUR

The Führer had given Bormann special orders—a special mission.

                              FRANK

What—sort of mission?

                                BAUR

I do not know. But it was vitally important to the Führer.

                              FRANK

Some say Martin Bormann survived.

                                BAUR
                      (a faraway look in his eyes)

I never did like Martin Bormann. No one did. He treated me well, but he was…difficult to read. No one trusted him. He determined the order in which we left the bunker.
                        (pauses, lost in thought)
Naumann took the lead; Bormann would follow; then Stumpfegger, then me. I had the Führer's favorite painting of Frederick the Great which he gave me before he died. It was rolled

up and strapped to my knapsack. We all ran out together but hardly reached the street when we were fired on. We made it to the Weidendamm Bridge, then ran along the Ziegelstrasse.
    (soft, directed at Frank)
It was an inferno, my boy. Pray God you will never see its like. Berlin, our beautiful city, was dying. Anyone who lived through that terrible time will never forget—the images of horror, suffering and destruction will return forever.
    (beat)
We were quickly scattered. I lost sight of Reichsleiter Bormann and never saw him again. I saw no one again. No one could have survived.

      FRANK

But *you* survived, Herr General?

      BAUR

I survived—just barely. And not all of me.
    (slaps his false leg)
I survived to spend ten years as a prisoner of the Russians.

His wife reaches over and puts her hand on his.

      BAUR

But Bormann is dead—dead and buried in some mass grave with all the others lying in the streets. No one would have recognized him. He is dead.

      FRANK

Could you have flown the Führer out of Berlin?

      BAUR
    (nods pensively)
Even on the night of April 29th, the day before *unser Vati* left us forever, I could have flown him to safety. He summoned me to tell me to leave. And to stay with Reichsleiter Bormann. I told the Führer we could still get out. I told him I could fly him to—to—anywhere. But he refused to leave.
    (looks soberly at Frank)
Perhaps if he had known what was in store for me, he would have let me stay, he would have let me follow him, as I always had.

      FRANK

But why did the Russians keep you for ten years? That wasn't normal. What did they want from you?

                         BAUR

To know where *unser Vati* was. They thought I knew. They
thought he was alive—and that I knew about…other things,
too.
                         (sighs)
I was constantly beaten, deprived of sleep, tortured. During
those years I often regretted I could not have stayed with *unser Vati* and shared his fate, his ultimate sacrifice for the Fatherland. It was what I wanted to do. And I would have, even
in Russia. But it is not easy to do away with yourself when
you are being watched. They found and took the small blade I
had honed from a piece of scrap iron. If I stopped eating, they
force-fed me. Day after day, a rough tube was forced through
my nose or my throat until everything was like bloody raw
meat. Even the Russian doctor, listening to me scream, had
tears in her eyes as she carried out her orders. When I passed
out from the pain, they fed me through the damned tube. So
you see, even a way out was denied me.

Baur turns away, the memories beginning to take their toll. He rises and walks over to the bust of Hitler where he stands motionless, his back to his wife and Frank.

                         BAUR

He was a great man. A great man, my boy. One of the greatest
the world will ever know.
                         (slowly he turns back)
If history had been written by anyone other than the enemies
of the Reich, *unser Vati* would have gone down in history as a
giant among men.

He walks back and sits next to his wife. Her head is bowed, hands in her lap over the box of chocolates on which she has been nibbling. Baur looks Frank straight in the eyes.

                         BAUR

If only you could have known him, as I did, you would have
agreed. The burdens placed on him were far greater than any
placed on me; his resolve much stronger. You talk about a
holocaust, a holocaust that never happened. If you are truly
researching the Hitler time, then you have already heard what
I am telling you now about the so-called holocaust.

Frank shifts uneasily.

FRANK
(stammering)
Well you see, Herr Flugkapitän, I…I *am* doing research, but you…you are the first person I have spoken to.

Baur stares for a moment, then laughs aloud. The Dachshund, asleep at his feet, wakes up and gives Frank a nasty look as if he's responsible for disturbing his nap.

BAUR
Then we must remedy that, must we not? I know a few people who I am certain can be of help to you.

FRANK
That would be most helpful of you, Herr Flugkapitän. Most kind.

BAUR
Let me see…there is Rudel, our most decorated war hero. I am sure you've heard of him.

Frank nods eagerly.

BAUR
He was in the bunker with us…There are others. Karl Wolff. Important men. They value their —eh, privacy, of course, but I will find out if they will talk to you.

Frank stands with a formal, polite nod to his host.

FRANK
I am most grateful, Herr Flugkapitän.

Baur stands.

BAUR
Schon gut. I shall try to send you the addresses of Rudel and Wolff. You will find them both interesting to talk to.
(to his wife)
Mutti, don't you think our young friend would like to have a piece of your *Apfelstrudel* to take along on his trip back to Munich? There will be plenty left for us.

Frau Baur plops another chocolate in her mouth and stands, smiling brightly.

FRAU BAUR
But of course, I shall wrap a large piece for Herr Brandenburg.

44   INT/EXT—S-BAHN RAPID TRANSIT (MOVING)—DAY

Frank leans back and watches the countryside go by, lost in thought, quietly munching on Frau Baur's *Apfelstrudel*.

45   INT. BRANDENBURG HOUSE—HALLWAY

Wilhelm watches from a doorway as Frank makes a series of calls to former Nazis. He catches only snatches of the names and conversations. Heim, Jordan, Lorenze…

>   FRANK
>   (into phone)
> *Flugkapitän* Baur suggested that I call you…Yes…I am doing
> research on…Oh—I see…Yes, I understand.

He hangs up and studies his list, dejected but not to be undone.

                                                           DISSOLVE TO:

46   INT. FRANK'S BEDROOM—BRANDENBURG HOUSE—LATER

Frank bends over his desk, intent on a letter. He signs it with a flourish, folds it, then reaches for a glossy PHOTO and places it in the envelope along with the letter.

                                                           DISSOLVE TO:

47   INT. BRANDENBURG HOUSE—FRANK'S BEDROOM (WEEKS LATER)

The door opens and Wilhelm enters, followed by Gritti. Gritti jumps up on the bed as Wilhelm hands Frank a letter.

>   WILHELM
>   (teasing him)
> From one of your…criminals.

Elated, Frank tears into the letter and reads.

>   LORENZ (V.O.)
> Most honored Mr. Brandenburg…Please understand I cannot
> comply with your request as a matter of course. I should like
> to know something of your background. How do you come
> into possession of the photograph you sent me? Do you col-
> lect these for historical purposes? Have you any connections
> with the right radical or so-called neo-Nazi circles…

Gritti BARKS and Frank looks up at his grandfather.

                    FRANK
        He won't see me, Gran'pa, but…he wants to know about me!

Wilhelm shakes his head and exits, saying nothing.

                    FRANK
                  (to Gritti)
        So, what do you think? It's not going to be as easy as I
        thought.

He stands and paces beneath pictures of antique automobiles, landscapes, a signed Dali lithograph, a yellow ceramic sun, and family photos. Finally, his eyes come to rest on a framed MOTTO. He steps up to it and reads, aloud:

                    FRANK
        A little more "we" and less of the "I"—a little more strength,
        not just "let it go by"…

He crosses to Gritti and gathers the small dog in his arms.

                    FRANK
                  (to Gritti)
        That's it, girl; not to "let it go by."

                                                              DISSOLVE TO:

48   INT. BRANDENBURG HOUSE—HALLWAY (WEEKS LATER)

Wilhelm, shuffling through the mail, hands Frank another letter.

                    WILHELM
              (teasing, but with a touch of disapproval)
        From your friend, Herr Criminal-gent Baur.

Frank grabs it, tears into it and begins to read.

                    BAUR (V.O.)
        Bormann ist tot und gefallen.

Startled, Frank looks up at his grandfather who is reading the letter over his shoulder.

                    WILHELM
        "Bormann is dead and fallen." Why does he write that? Every-
        one knows Bormann is dead.

Frank dives back into the letter and scans it quickly.

                    FRANK
                (to Wilhelm)
    He has given me names and addresses, Opa.
                (reading)
    Ministerialdirigent Henrich Heim, Ungarerstrasse, Munich;
    Reichsstatthalter, Gauleiter Rudolf Jordan, St. Paul Strasse,
    Munich; and SS Oberstgruppenführer…Karl Wolff, Wil-
    helminenstrasse, Darmstadt!
                (looks up, eyes wide)
    Karl Wolff, Opa.

Wilhelm waves one hand as if fending off the name.

                    WILHELM
                (suddenly serious)
    Karl Wolff was—a war criminal, Frank. Convicted.

                    FRANK
    And he was the personal adjutant to Himmler. He was every-
    where. Knew everything. I will write this Karl Wolff—a little
    better letter this time.

                                                    DISSOLVE TO:

49 INT. KITCHEN—BRANDENBURG HOUSE—MORNING

Frank's entire family is seated around the breakfast table as he walks through carrying his duffel bag and a three-foot cardboard cylinder. He stops to nod a polite good-bye to a wall of silence, then continues on. When he reaches the door, his father calls out.

                    KARL-PETER
                (to Frank's back)
    Call us from Darmstadt.
                (Beat)
    Frank? Did you hear me?

Frank stops at the door, turns.

                    FRANK
    Yes, papa.

He exits. All look from one to the other, concerned.

50 INT/EXT. TRAIN (MOVING)—DAY

Ice has formed on the windows of the train. Frank shivers even in his coat and blows on the glass.

Frank checks his watch, then removes a fresh shirt and pants from his duffel bag. At the same time he examines his tape recorder and notices it is in the "on" position. Damn. He checks it, shakes it—nothing. He rolls his eyes.

> FRANK
> Great! General Wolff…and the batteries in my tape recorder are dead!

He stuffs the tape recorder back into the bag, then rises and carries his clothes to the back of the car.

51   INT. TRAIN RESTROOM

In the freezing cold, Frank removes sweatshirt and jeans and struggles into his best clothes for his meeting with General Wolff. The restroom is small, cramped and surreal, like a prison interrogation room.

52   INT/EXT. TRAIN (MOVING)—SAME DAY

Back in his seat, Frank checks his image in the train window as objects pass by—trees, buildings, overpasses. Their shadows on the glass allow him to see himself—to straighten his tie, comb his hair. He settles back nervously.

53   EXT. HOUSE—WILHELMINENSTRASSE—DARMSTADT—DAY

FRANK walks into the shot to stand before the door, juggling his duffel bag and a three-foot long cardboard tube. He manages to knock on the door.

A plain woman with straw-blonde hair in a straight bob presently opens the door.

> FRANK
> *Guten Tag, gnädige Frau.* I am Frank Brandenburg.

> WOMAN
> I am Edeltraut Ziegmann, a friend of Herr Wolff's. This way, please.

She ushers him in.

54   INT. LIVING ROOM—ZIEGMANN'S HOUSE—CONTINUOUS

Frank follows Frau Ziegmann into the room where a massive gold chandelier hangs over a life-size, gold-framed, full-figure painting of Wolff in SS uniform.

As Frank tears his eyes from the portrait, he is suddenly aware of a slight MAN with thinning hair and an elongated face sunk in a chair across the room. The Man rises and comes slowly towards him.

                    FRAU ZIEGMANN
          Herr Brandenburg, this is Otto mumble, mumble—
                    (unintelligible last name; back to Frank)
          Please—have a seat.

All three sit for an awkward moment, then Frau Ziegmann breaks the silence.

                    FRAU ZIEGMANN
                    (re tube)
          May I ask, Herr Brandenburg, what it is you have in that container?

                    FRANK
          A picture. A rolled-up picture. A little gift for the Herr General.

                    FRAU ZIEGMANN
          May we see it?

He hands it over and she and Otto examine it—hefting it, peering at the folded-in ends.

As they're checking it, Frank notices an electric plug on the floor; relieved, he whips out a cord, plugs in his tape recorder and turns it on to charge it for his interview.

Otto hands the tube back and Frau Ziegmann smiles.

                    FRAU ZIEGMANN
          How old are you, Herr Brandenburg?

                    FRANK
          Nearly…uh, twenty.

He lies. Frau Ziegmann smiles.

                    FRAU ZIEGMANN
          And how did you come to know General Wolff's address and telephone number?

                    FRANK
          Flugkapitän General Hans Baur gave them to me…when I visited him in Herrsching.

She and Otto exchange an approving glance.

                    FRAU ZIEGMANN
          And why do you wish to speak with General Wolff?

FRANK

I am interested in the time of the Third Reich, Frau Ziegmann. I am doing research on it. I have read a lot, but everything is so—confusing. It is difficult to learn the facts. The truth. So I thought…I could learn a lot if I could talk to someone important and knowledgeable—someone who *really* knows. Like Flugkapitän Baur. Or General Wolff.

He smiles, sure he has pulled it off. Frau Ziegmann will now be eating out of his hand. But no, she continues her hard line.

FRAU ZIEGMANN

Are you alone, Herr Brandenburg, or do you have…associates?

FRANK

Oh—alone.

FRAU ZIEGMANN

Are you a journalist? A reporter?

FRANK

No, I—

CLICK. Frau Ziegmann and Otto jump, their eyes dart towards the bag. Otto rises.

OTTO

What was that!?

FRANK

Oh, I'm sorry. It's nothing. The tape recorder ran out, that's all. I'll—I'll just turn the tape.

OTTO/FRAU ZIEGMANN
(in unison)

Tape recorder!

FRANK

Oh, it'll only take a second…

Suddenly Otto is beside him, reaching down, yanking the cord from the wall.

OTTO

You will not record while you are here! Is that clear? And what else do you have in that bag?

                              FRANK
                Uh…laundry. Some books, my camera…

Frau Ziegmann breaks in mercifully, motioning for Otto to sit down.

                           FRAU ZIEGMANN
                You said, Herr Baur. Did Herr Baur give you any *other*
                names?

Grateful that he won't have to show his dirty laundry, Frank launches into a list of names—names that roll easily off his tongue.

                              FRANK
                Ministerialdirigent Heinrich Heim, Reichsstatthälter, Gauleiter Rudolf Jordan—and Luftwaffeadjutant Nicholaus von Below. And Rudel. The Luftwaffe ace, Oberst Hans Ulrich Rudel.

A voice answers from out of the shadows.

                           MAN'S VOICE (O.S.)
                You will find Colonel Rudel quite a formidable man, Herr
                Brandenburg. I can vouch for that.

Frank turns to see SS Oberstgruppenführer KARL WOLFF.

Wolff, 81, stands erect, an imposing figure, tall and well built. His hair is silver, his face craggy and etched with deep wrinkles. He is wearing a dark suit with an open shirt and no tie.

SUPER: KARL WOLFF

Frank stands up, in awe, as Wolff strides over and extends his hand. Frank shakes it. Wolff turns to Otto.

                              WOLFF
                Thank you, Otto. That will be all.

Otto slinks out and Wolff turns his full attention to Frank.

                              WOLFF
                You must forgive me. First for not answering your kind letter.
                Letter writers seem to be legion these days and one simply
                can't answer them all.
                              (re sofa)
                Please, sit.

He sits beside Frau Ziegmann and Frank returns to the sofa.

The Brandenburg Quest   31.

                            WOLFF
And second for subjecting you to that little…interrogation.
Unfortunately, it is necessary to be cautious.
                    (off Frank's quizzical look)
You could have been a Mossad agent, Herr Brandenburg. Israeli agents are everywhere.
                    (laughs, then grows sober)
Fact is, I *have* had threats. More than once.
                    (leans forward)
Now. How can I help you?

Frank hesitates a moment, not wanting to make a mistake.

                            FRANK
General Wolff…In my research, I have found much that is contradictory. A few years ago, I saw a film on television: The Holocaust. I am trying to find out the truth about it. Did it happen that way? And so I am talking to the men in Germany who would know best. The most powerful men of those times.

Wolff leans in close, his grey-blue eyes disturbingly penetrating.

                            WOLFF
The concentration camps did exist. It cannot be denied, but most were work or resettlement camps to which men and women were…transferred from specific areas to offer relief from intolerable situations. But…
                    (a dark look crosses his face)
In other camps, certain… 'people' *were* afforded special treatment: their numbers 'reduced' as it were. But certainly not to the exaggerated extent some claim today. Personally, I *had nothing* to *do with* these camps.
                    (holds up his hand as if anticipating Frank's protest)
I know what you are thinking. I have heard it before from others. Yes, I was convicted and imprisoned for those very crimes. But you must not believe everything you hear or read, or see. Often things are not what they seem. Was I guilty? No, my only guilt was in doing my duty. And I never had anything to do with the killing of the Jews. My duties involved many things, but never that. However…
                    (spreads his hands, as if weighing his culpability)
…the court chose to believe the lies put out by the international Jewish community. It was the "fad" of the times—and I became one of its victims.

Frank settles in. Wolff seems so logical, so plausible. What he's saying could be true; in fact, it probably is. Wolff continues:

> WOLFF
> In fact, it is known that I helped many Jews leave Germany when life here became…difficult for them.
> (proudly)
> One of them was the world-renowned banker, Baron Louis de Rothschild. That is even part of the Nürnberg trial records. Does that sound like the deed of a war criminal?

Frank shakes his head, no, but he does wonder what Rothschild must have paid in exchange for this help.

Suddenly, he remembers the poster and offers it to Wolff.

> FRANK
> Please, I took the liberty of bringing you a small gift. I hope you will like it.

Wolff is taken aback, startled—like a child at Christmas.

> WOLFF
> How very thoughtful of you.

He pulls it out of the tube, then spreads it on a table. He stares at it awhile, a faraway look on his face, then looks over at Frank, eyes brimming with tears.

55   CLOSE SHOT

We see the picture.

BACK TO SCENE

> WOLFF
> Those were wonderful days, my young friend. Wonderful days. How very, very thoughtful of you!

> FRANK
> It is my pleasure, Herr General.

Wolff settles back down and studies Frank a beat.

> WOLFF
> There must be something besides the Jewish question you would like to know.

FRANK
Yes…one more thing, Herr General. Reichsführer Himmler did not survive but others did. I am interested in knowing if Reichsleiter Martin Bormann did. Survive.

Frau Ziegmann sits bolt upright and cries out, her voice growing more strident with each cry.

FRAU ZIEGMANN
Bormann is dead. He is dead, he is dead, he is dead! There is nothing more to say.

Wolff leans over and pats her hand, speaking softly.

WOLFF
Schon gut, Edeltraut, schon gut.
(turns to Frank)
There are some things it is not wise to discuss.

He stands, signaling the end of the interview. Frank rises too.

FRANK
Thank you, Herr General. It was kind of you to see me.

Wolff takes Frank's hand in both of his.

WOLFF
(sincere)
It was my pleasure, Frank.

FRANK
(nods to Frau Ziegmann)
Gnädige Frau.

He makes a short bow and she responds with a slight nod.

Wolff walks him out—past the imposing portrait of himself. Like Wolff in real life, it dominates the room.

WOLFF
Perhaps we shall meet again. Perhaps another time we shall discuss…other matters. When we know each other a little better, yes?

FRANK
I would be honored. You are most kind.

                    WOLFF
        Nonsense. It is my pleasure.

He opens the front door, then stops him.

                    WOLFF
                     (low)
        One more thing. If you are interested in Reichsleiter Bormann, you might talk to Heim—Heinrich Heim. He lives in Munich, in the Schwabing district on Ungarerstrasse, I believe.
                 (looks closely at Frank)
        He was Bormann's adjutant. And Hans Baur *did* mention him to you. *Ja?*
                     (beat)
        You might find Heinrich Heim very…interesting.

56   INT. TRAIN (MOVING)—NIGHT

Frank is writing in a notebook, recording his conversation with Wolff…

                    WOLFF (V.O.)
        —If you are interested in Reichsleiter Bormann you might like to talk to Heim—Heinrich Heim—Bormann's Adjutant—

57   EXT. MUNICH—AIR RAID SHELTER—DAY

Frank knocks on the iron door of an old air raid shelter. The door is opened a crack by HENRICH HEIM, 81, an unimpressive man with white hair, pale blue eyes and a fleshy face that looks remarkably robust for his age.

SUPER: HEINRICH HEIM

Heim is clad in a simple shabby, slate-gray suit with a loose black tie at his throat.

                    FRANK
        Ministerialdirigent Heim? Heinrich Heim?

Heim nods and opens the door, motioning him in.

INT. AIR RAID SHELTER—CONTINUOUS

Frank enters the windowless "bunker"—Heim's office. The small space is cluttered: stacks of paper, documents and file folders cover every surface; battered filing cabinets, a white-painted desk with an orange clamp-on lamp.

An open fuse box hangs on unpainted concrete walls while, in a prominent spot, the only color in the room jumps out: a picture from a magazine of a smiling ELVIS PRESLEY.

Frank reacts with a touch of panic as the heavy iron door CLANGS shut behind him.

Heim sits, motioning for Frank to do so, then waves a hand about himself and his surroundings.

> HEIM
> In my home I have more than twenty of the best suits money can buy. But I elect to stay here, and to wear what I do—in memory of the disgrace of having lost the war!
> (a mirthless smile)
> As a matter of fact, I like it here. I call it my cave.

DISSOLVE TO:

Heim steeples his fingers and taps them together.

> HEIM
> I had no knowledge of what has been claimed about what you call the Holocaust, young man. I did not learn of these claims until after the war. I do not even think A.H. had knowledge of anything like what is claimed to have happened.

> FRANK
> You were Reichsleiter Bormann's adjutant for three years. General Wolff told me you may have some documents written by him.

> HEIM
> Did he?

> FRANK
> Yes. Do you?

Heim contemplates him pensively, steeples his fingers again and taps them together.

> HEIM
> As you undoubtedly know, young man, M.B. gave me the task of compiling and recording the speeches and remarks made by A.H. at various meetings and functions. My reports span the time from 1941 through 1944. But I do have a few pages, unpublished—fifty or sixty of them—notes dictated by M.B. for the month of February 1945. Just before…the end.

FRANK (O.C.)
Why did you not put them in your book?

HEIM
Suffice it to say, I did not.

Heim gets up and crosses to a bookcase, pulls out a records box, opens it, and takes out a sheaf of papers about an inch thick. He hands them to Frank who takes them eagerly and leafs through them. He scans a page.

FRANK (V.O.)
(reading, to himself)
"One day Germany will emerge from this struggle stronger than ever!"
(his eyes light on another passage)
"I deliberately spared the British at Dunkirk, but Churchill was too stupid to recognize my gesture of good will."

Frank looks up, amazed at what Hein has shown him.

FRANK
May I keep these—long enough to read them?

HEIM
You may have them.

He sits back down. Frank is stunned, delighted.

FRANK
(emboldened by Heim's generosity)
Do you think Reichsleiter Bormann survived the breakout from the bunker?

Heim rises from his chair.

HEIM
There are some things it is unwise to discuss.
(walks over to Frank)
Perhaps you will call, or visit me again. Later. Perhaps we can then…talk. Later. Meanwhile…you will keep our conversation confidential.

Frank rise and moves towards the door.

FRANK
You have been most generous with your time, Herr Heim. Most generous. Only…one more question, if I may. Forgive me but…

The Brandenburg Quest

> (motions to wall)
> …why do you have a picture of Elvis Presley on your wall?

> HEIM
> (glances back at wall, then back to Frank)
> Oh, that. The granddaughter of a friend gave it to me; obviously one of her treasures. He seems like a pleasant enough young man. I put it up to please her.
> (beat)
> Who *is* Elvis Presley?

58 INT. BRANDENBURG HOUSE—FRANK'S BUNKER

Frank's office "bunker" for his ever growing research, is a former fruit cellar lined with paneled walls, a floor of carpet remnants, and old furniture: a grandfather clock; an oak cupboard for his Nazi paraphernalia; a desk, a table and three chairs.

Frank and his father drag in a heavy bookcase and set it up along one wall. Boxes of books lie scattered about waiting to be placed on shelves. Frank looks about proudly.

On the wall behind the desk is a POSTER of ADOLF HITLER along with two framed and autographed PHOTOS of Wolff and Baur.

In a cupboard, he has PHOTOS of himself and those he's met, or wants to—many autographed.

> FRANK
> Thank you, father.

Karl-Peter looks around and shakes his head.

> KARL-PETER
> Thank your grandmother. I never thought I'd live to see the day her fruit cellar was turned into a Nazi… "bunker."

Frank crosses to his desk and turns on a tape recorder. The room is suddenly flooded with the lush strains of WAGNER.

> FRANK
> You do approve of Wagner?

> KARL-PETER
> I have nothing against Wagner. It is the rest of this—
> (motions around him)
> …I disapprove of.

He turns to go.

                    FRANK
Well, Opa doesn't feel that way.

                    KARL-PETER
                    (turns back)
Your grandfather has memories of all this. Thank God…*we* don't.

WAGNER PLAYS…

                                        DISSOLVE TO:

59   EXT. STIMMER LAKE—VILLA REFUGIUM—DAY

WAGNER continues on the cassette player of the rental car as Frank drives the hills above Stimmer Lake and the surrounding green mountains of the Tyrol. Farmers work, plowing the fields.

Frank drives up to a beautifully landscaped two-story Tyrolean villa, REFUGIUM. Het gets out, carrying his duffel bag and a nicely packaged bottle of wine.

At the door, he presses the button on the security system and identifies himself. He is BUZZED in.

60   INT. VILLA REFUGIUM—DAY

Luftwaffe Oberst HANS-ULRICH RUDEL—most decorated soldier in WWII—tilts his head back and laughs.

SUPER: LUFTWAFFE OBERST, HANS-ULRICH RUDEL

Still handsome at 65, Rudel wears a casual short-sleeved, open-necked white shirt and light blue slacks.

A totally unrepentant Nazi, Rudel jabs a finger at Frank from time to time to accentuate his points as he talks.

                    RUDEL
It was a *film, lieber Herr* Brandenburg. A clumsy motion picture, designed by those who wish us ill, to show Germany and the Nazis in a bad light. You must remember…our enemies hate National Socialism because it exalts the superior qualities of the German people. That… "Holocaust" spectacle of yours had nothing to do with reality, nothing at all; those… extermination camps pictured on the screen never existed. What you saw was nothing but fanciful fiction—and one must be careful not to take as truth such distortions. The concentration camps depicted by the Allies are a myth. A lie.

The Brandenburg Quest

The room, light and airy with a grand view of the mountains, is filled with MEDALS and TROPHIES, along with several large paintings of Rudel.

>   RUDEL
> So you see, much of what you hear, *mein lieber Herr Brandenburg*, is untrue. Lies.
>   (stands)
> I am being a poor host. You were kind enough to bring me a bottle of good German wine. The least we can do is sample it.

He brings two glasses over, opens the bottle of Rhine wine Frank has bought, and pours.

>   FRANK
> You knew the Führer well?

>   RUDEL
> I should have liked to know him better. He was a genius. A true genius. One of the greatest geniuses the world has ever known. Mark my words, *lieber Herr Brandenburg*, one day the world will recognize this. One day the world will speak in a different way about the Third Reich than it does today.
>   (raises his glass in a toast)
> *Zum Wohl!* I promise you.

Frank joins in the toast.

>   FRANK
> Herr Oberst, you spent several years in South America after the war.

>   RUDEL
> Good years, with many good friends.

>   FRANK
> German?

Rudel settles back into his chair.

>   RUDEL
> Of course.

>   FRANK
> How did they get out of Germany?

>   RUDEL
> The various escape routes.
>   (lights a cigarette)

Are you interested in how we took care of our own? Really interested?

FRANK

Very.

Rudel takes a long drag on his cigarette before he speaks.

RUDEL

Already in mid-1944, wise heads in Berlin realized the day would come when many of the most important men would be forced into hiding to escape the vengeance of the Allies, and that hiding within Germany would be impossible. Refuge would have to be sought abroad.
 (he lights a new cigarette with the old one)
And that was the beginning. The first step was to provide those needing assistance with false papers: passports, identity cards, birth certificates, marriage licenses. These were prepared by secret groups set up by the SS and the Gestapo, such as Operation Birch Tree. But since the papers were prepared by the authorities with official stamps, they were not really forgeries as such, you see. They were foolproof.

FRANK (O.C.)

What were these escape routes?

RUDEL

At first, the most active and important were *Die Schleuse* and *Die Spinne*—*La Arana* in Spain and *L'Araignee* in France. Die Spinne—the Spider—ran the B-B Axis and—
 (off Frank's puzzled look)
—So called because the route began in *Bremen* and ended in *Bari*, southern Italy. After the war another took over—most effective of all: ODESSA. Eichmann used it. Its headquarters moved for security purposes: first Stuttgart, then Augsburg, Munich, with branches all over—Germany, Austria, South America. Two main routes: Bremen to Rome and Bremen to Genoa, with a third "escape" hatch through Flensburg to Denmark, and on from there. It was financed from accounts hidden in countries like Switzerland…

Rudel takes a deep drag on his cigarette and lets the smoke out with a subtle smile…

RUDEL

…as well as large hoards of money and valuables, uh—contributed by the Jews and hidden right here in this country.

The Brandenburg Quest

Ingenious, no? And it hid behind groups with *clever* names: Aid and Mutual Interest League, Silent Aid, Brotherhood. In Austria, the Salzburg Circle. St. Martin's Fund in Belgium, The Danish Alliance of Front Fighters, Aid Organization for War Wounded…And so on. You see? No one thought twice about it. People hear what they want to hear. Words can be used to make them feel safe.

FRANK

And your own group, Herr Oberst, *nicht wahr*?

RUDEL

And my own: *Der Rudel Klub*. In Argentina. You have done your homework, I see.

Frank smiles and tosses off the next question as if it were no big deal.

FRANK

Did Martin Bormann get out?

Rudel throws him a quick look.

RUDEL

He did.

Frank sucks in his breath.

FRANK

Do you know how he got out?

RUDEL
(off-handed)

The Vatican—with the International Red Cross, helped many Germans who were anti-Communist or Catholic reach South America with a special escape route, the Vatican Aid Line, known also as the Monastery Route. South American countries were Catholic, you see, so the Vatican could exert a certain…influence. Bormann used the Monastery Route, over the Alps at Nauders, staying in many safe-houses, then on to Rome.

He leans forward, intent on Frank, studying him a beat.

RUDEL

You seem to be genuinely interested in the old times. We need such interest. We welcome it. You seem to be the kind of young man we would like to know better. Of course your attitude in some things could be a little more…enthusiastic. Still, if, or rather, *when* I go back to South America, would you like to come with me? For a short stay. Many are still there. Klaus Barbie, Walter Kutschmann, Walter Fauff. Mengele was there.

Frank starts.

                            FRANK
Mengele? The one they call the Angel of Death? From Auschwitz?

                            RUDEL
                            (scoffs)
That ridiculous epithet. Of course, I knew him—

He breaks off and studies Frank for a moment, then gets up and walks slowly to the picture-glass window. Outside, it has begun to rain. The distant mountains are shrouded in slow-moving clouds.

                            RUDEL
I think I have just told you something I should not have…
Why don't we take a nice walk, you and I. We can talk.
                        (nods towards mountains)
Out there—we can be alone.

He walks toward the door. On the way he picks up a double barrelled shotgun. He loads it, and gun-motions Frank to follow him. They leave.

Frank's swallows hard and stifles his fear.

61   EXT. MOUNTAINSIDE PATH—DAY

Frank trudges along wearing Rudel's rainboots—at least one size too large—and an oversized raincoat. He tries to fight the fear creeping up on him as they go further and further into the wilderness.

A soft rain falls. Rudel turns his face up toward the gentle drizzle and speaks rapturously.

                            RUDEL
Nectar of the mountains, Herr Brandenburg. The mist from the Fountain of Youth itself…
                        (his voice turns oddly menacing)
A man could—lose himself—in that mist.

62   EXT. THICKET—MOUNTAINSIDE—CONTINUOUS—DAY

They enter the thicket. Rudel stop, turns to Frank—his gun held before him. Suddenly he raises it—and fires both shots into the air. Frank starts.

> RUDEL
> That should make them think I've gone pheasant hunting.

He reloads the gun, turns to Frank, the gun before him, his manner suddenly cold and harsh.

> Now, Herr Brandenburg. The truth. Who are you? Really? More to the point *what* are you?

> FRANK
> I—I am—Frank Branden—

> RUDEL
> (briskly)
> What do you really want?

> FRANK
> Information. Only information. I—

> RUDEL
> Why?

> FRANK
> I—I am interested. I only called you because General Wolff suggested—

> RUDEL
> Wolff? You know Karl Wolff?

> FRANK
> Yes, I—

> RUDEL
> How?

> FRANK
> I—I met him. I—

> RUDEL
> Where?

> FRANK
> At his home. In Darmstadt. On Wilhelmstrasse. With a man called Otto. And Frau Ziegmann.

Rudel's attitude changes. He places his gun against a tree.

> RUDEL
> I have been there myself, Herr Brandenburg.
> (he savors the memory)
> A very—comfortable room. And that great bronze-sculptured eagle in the corner. Magnificent, don't you think?

Frank is taken aback, uneasy.

> FRANK
> Well—I—I don't remember—an eagle. I—

RUDEL laughs.

> RUDEL
> No wonder! There IS no such sculpture!

FRANK blushes at the realization he had been tested.

RUDEL walks to a fallen tree trunk, and sits down. He motions for Frank to join him.

> RUDEL
> So—you want to talk about the old times. The times of glory, of pride and patriotism. *Schon gut.*
> (He looks around)
> This will do. We should be safe from eavesdroppers here.
> (laughs)
> For want of a better word, you may think me melodramatic, but I have good reason to believe that certain…agents watch my house with strong binoculars, hoping to read my lips. Here, no one can see us talk.

See us talk? Frank doesn't know whether to laugh—or to run for his life. And so he says nothing as he waits for Rudel to reveal his purpose for bringing him out here—to pull a gun on him or to tell him a secret.

> RUDEL
> (jovial)
> You picked up on my little slip quickly enough. So I shall take you into my confidence with all the risks that entails—and a warning that what you learn should be held in the strictest confidence.

Frank nods eagerly, making sure Rudel knows he agrees.

                    RUDEL (CONT'D)
          The truth is—
                    (a suspenseful beat)
          —Mengele is dead.

Frank stares at him, but doesn't dare blink. That's it? That's why he brought him here?

                    FRANK
          I assure you, Herr Oberst, I will say nothing about it. But—
          may I ask—why? Why is it so important to keep it—a secret?

Rudel gives him a thin smile.

                    RUDEL
          The more people who waste their time looking for Mengele,
          the fewer are looking for others in hiding. And we want to
          keep it that way. We are tying up the enemy forces on a wild
          goose chase, and that is an excellent strategy, *nicht wahr*?

                    FRANK
          Ah…I see—

A blinding flash of LIGHTNING slashes the sky, followed by a clap of THUNDER. The heavens open up.

63   INT. RUDEL'S VILLA REFUGIUM (DAY)

Frank and Rudel sit before a roaring fire, warming themselves. Frank wears a borrowed shirt and pants while his own clothes dry. His hair is still soaking wet.

FRAU RUDEL, a pleasant woman in her late 40s, enters with coffee and cookies.

64   CLOSE ON—FIRE

                    RUDEL (O.C.)
          Your desire to meet and talk to as many of us old-timers as
          you can is commendable and interesting, *mein lieber Herr
          Brandenburg*.

During the following Mrs. Rudel enters with a vase of flowers which she arranges on a table.

                    RUDEL
          And there are *many* of us around. Not men defeated and dis-
          heartened, but men still proud and impassioned. My motto
          has always been: "Only he is lost, who gives up on himself."
          Many of us have not given up—and never will!

CAMERA ZOOMS IN onto the FLOWERS.

65 EXT. HILDESHEIM OPEN MARKET—FLOWER STAND—DAY

FLOWERS. Frank prepares a bouquet. Ilse stands to one side, watching.

> FRANK
> They're for his wife. And even if he doesn't have a wife, everyone likes flowers, don't you think?

> ILSE
> Such…foolishness! To feed the lions flowers and chocolates. These men are not nice men.

> FRANK
> I'm just being a good son. Polite, like you taught me to be.

He picks out a purple ribbon.

> FRANK
> A good color for a Generalmajor, yes?
> (tying the ribbon)
> And besides…if they're as bad as you say, why are they still here—in Germany—serving strudel with silver tongs from the past. Well?

Ilse folds her arms and says nothing. Frank finishes tying the ribbon with a flourish, grabs his duffel bag and smiles.

66 CLOSE ON—FLOWERS

DISSOLVE TO:

67 INT. REMER'S APARTMENT—LIVING ROOM

FLOWERS. In FRANK'S hands. CAMERA PANS the room to where Generalmajor OTTO ERNST REMER stands, ramrod straight, watching Frank.

…an imposing form surrounded by MEDALS, DECORATIONS, BOOKS on the Third Reich, a gleaming gray *STAHLHELM*: a STEEL HELMET with the black-white-and-red insignia of the Wehrmacht.

SUPER: GENERALMAJOR OTTO ERNST REMER

A tall, slender man, legs slightly apart, hands behind his back, chin high, Remer still has the ramrod-straight bearing of a German officer; he has receding gray hair and blue eyes, eerily magnified in large horn-rimmed glasses; he is clad in a gray suit and open-neck white shirt.

                              REMER
          Brandenburg, I trust you have not brought those flowers for
          me.

He points a stiff finger at the flowers Frank clutches in his hands.

                              FRANK
          Oh, no, Herr General! I—they—are for Frau Remer.
                    (presents them, with a bow)
          Bitte, gnädige Frau…

                              FRAU REMER
          Thank you, I shall put them in water.

She leaves. Remer points to a straight-backed chair.

                              REMER
          Sit down.

He remains standing, towering over Frank. He lights a cigarette.

                              REMER
          Why are we here?

                              FRANK
          I wanted—uh—Colonel Rudel suggested I talk with you.

                              REMER
          Why?

                              FRANK
          I—I am doing research on the Third Reich, Herr General, and
          I—

                              REMER
          Why?

                              FRANK
          I am interested in the time. I want to know exactly what it
          was like. I—

                              REMER
          Why?

                              FRANK
          So much has been said about it. I want to know what is true
          and what is not.

                            REMER
Such as?

                            FRANK
Well…they talk about the Holocaust—

                            REMER
Nonsense!
              (jabs his cigarette at Frank)
Absurd exaggeration. What else?

Frau Remer walks by, the flowers arranged neatly in a blue and white vase. She sets it down and takes a seat, politely, as her husband begins a long, and at times terrifying, finger-jabbing lecture directed at Frank.

                            REMER
You come here, Brandenburg, presenting yourself as a serious researcher, but you ask me a frivolous, banal question.
I can answer with platitudes. The Holocaust is a lie. I can tell you that Germany should get out of that insidious NATO organization. I can tell you that I elected to remain in Germany rather than join my friends in South America, because I *am* and *feel* German. I can tell you I advocate a strong army of Arabs and their German friends to fight and destroy the oppressive international Jewry, and to put an end to the inhuman atrocities committed by the Jews in the Middle East. Platitudes. Banalities. I repeat—I can tell you all that…
              (ominous)
…but that is not why you are here, is it, Brandenburg?

Frank stiffens. Remer doesn't wait for an answer.

                            REMER
I am certain you know that after the war I founded the Socialist Reich Party. They called it neo-Nazi. It was not. It was Nazi. I repeat—Nazi! So it was outlawed. And I am also certain you know I am the leader of *Der Bismarck-Deutsche*, the club for right-thinking people who, like Bismarck himself, fight for our right to exist, for the security and freedom of a united Germany. People like me, Brandenburg. And like you…right? *That* is the reason you are here, *nicht wahr*? To learn what you can about us? To join us? That is why Rudel sent you to me. Am I right, Brandenburg? Am I right?
              (he stops and changes gears)
Ours is the fight for German liberty. Germany must be strong, as it was under Bismarck. That is why our club carries

The Brandenburg Quest   49.

his name. Since the war, a fight has raged, a fight for justice, for truth and for freedom of the German people, and we of *Der Bismarck-Deutsche stand in the forefront of that fight. And you, Brandenburg, want to stand with us. Right?*

Frank is seized by a moment of panic and hesitates. What to do? He decides to be political rather than risk cutting off his sources.

FRANK

You are right, Herr General. I am interested in learning more about *Der Bismarck-Deutsche*, and I—

He is saved by Remer's intense need to dominate everything.

REMER

Gut! I will get you some literature. And an application.

He rises and crosses to a desk. Frau Remer stands, suddenly cheery.

FRAU REMER

I think is about time we had a nice cup of coffee. And perhaps some nice crackers. You do like crackers, Herr Brandenburg?

FRANK
(nods)

Bitte.

Remer returns and hands Frank the application form. Frank takes it, looks it over, then looks up.

FRANK

Herr General, you spoke of your friends in South America. Are you still in touch with them?

REMER

Of course!

FRANK

Colonel Rudel mentioned some of them to me. Klaus Barbie, Walter Rauff, Walter Kurschmann. I suppose you know them too?

REMER

I do.

FRANK

And Martin Bormann?

Remer gives him a sharp look, then reaches over and slaps the application form in Frank's hand.

> REMER
> (curtly)
> Fill it out. Sent it in. And then we will deal with your questions.

Frau Remer interrupts carrying a tray. Business over, she serves crackers and coffee.

68 INT. HILDESHEIM—BOOK STORE—DAY

Frank spreads a collection of autographed photos out on the counter. The BOOKSELLER looks them over, impressed.

> FRANK
> I assure you, Herr Hoffman, the autographs are authentic.
> (pause)
> I cannot sell them myself, I am still…a student.

> BOOKSELLER
> And you want me to break the law?

> FRANK
> I am a poor student. I need to sell them to…finance my research. You are not breaking the law.

The Bookseller holds one up to the light.

> BOOKSELLER
> Hans Baur, the old rascal.
> (another and another)
> Rudel. Wolff. Nice. They will fetch a good price.
> (shakes his head)
> "Long time passing…" eh, Herr Brandenburg? You know the song?
> (smiles)
> How much?

> FRANK
> *Danke*, Herr Hoffman.

69 INT. BRANDENBURG HOUSE—FRANK'S BUNKER

Frank sits at his desk, feet up, sorting through his autograph collection, pleased with himself.

A knock on the door. Wilhelm cracks it.

> WILHELM
> (excited)
> He is here.

Frank stands quickly, hiding the autographs in a drawer and straightening his desk. The door opens and Frank turns to face his guest.

Karl Wolff steps inside, tears in his eyes as he looks around the room at the Third Reich mementos: the photos on the bare cement walls, the swastika-adorned people's radio, the Berghof letter folder once owned by Hitler, the portrait of the Führer.

> WOLFF
> *Ach, du lieber Gott!* This is just like stepping into yesterday.
> Into the glorious past.

Wilhelm leaves, discreetly closing the door behind him. A joyful Wolff turns his attention to Frank.

> WOLFF
> I almost expect the Führer to join us any moment.

He walks through the room, lovingly examining each object.

> WOLFF
> *Mein lieber*, Frank…you have created a small piece of history, a haven for memories.

He walks over to the bookshelf and takes out a copy of *Mein Kampf*.

> WOLFF
> I have not seen a copy of this for years.
> (he clasps it to his heart and recites from memory)
> "Just as the State of the People must devote the greatest attention to the training of the will and the strength of decision, it must, from an early age, implant the joy of responsibility and the courage of acceptance—
> (looks straight at Frank)
> —in the hearts of youth"
> (smiles)
> Those were the words of the Führer.

DISSOLVE TO:

Wolff sits opposite Frank at his desk, gently stroking the fork and spoon from the Osteria Bavaria restaurant. He sets them down and pulls out a nearby book from the bookcase. At the sight of it, he smiles a sardonic smile.

>WOLFF
>
>*The Bormann Brotherhood.* You read everything it appears.

He turns the book over in his hands. Frank seizes the moment.

>FRANK
>
>Yes, I do. And—I once asked you, Herr General, if Martin Bormann died in Berlin or survived to escape. I—I had the impression you would tell me—at a later date.
>>(pause)
>
>Did he survive?

Wolff gives him an amused little smile.

>WOLFF
>
>If you keep digging deep enough, my friend, you might unearth his bones. Or his ghost.

>FRANK
>
>Is he really a ghost? Or did he survive?

Wolff puts the book back with an impatient shove.

>WOLFF
>>(testily)
>
>Of course he survived. Of course he escaped. I did not tell you that the first time. Edeltraut does not want me to talk about it. To anyone.

>FRANK
>
>But why not?

>WOLFF
>
>It could have unpleasant consequences.
>>(firm)
>
>We will not discuss this any further. There are some things which could become dangerous for you to know.

Matter closed! An awkward silence follows.

>FRANK
>
>I have some nice wine. Perhaps you would like a glass of wine? We could listen to some music. I have some wonderful Wagner tapes.

Wolff visibly relaxes.

> **WOLFF**
> Ah, Wagner. By all means, Wagner.

DISSOLVE TO:

Wolff and Frank listen to Wagner and sip wine.

> **WOLFF**
> Hitler himself eulogized Reinhard Heydrich, calling him "the man with the iron heart whose name will resound with the greatest of heroes."
> (beat)
> Heydrich was the Führer's Aryan ideal. Of course this was a problem for him too. You understand?

> **FRANK**
> The Führer was jealous?

> **WOLFF**
> Everyone was jealous. But what could they do to the "poster boy" of their ideals?
> (motions to wall)
> Heydrich should be there. His wife, a beautiful woman, is still alive, I believe. Lina…
> (trying to remember)
> Lina, Lina, Lina—Manninen. That's it. She married again. A Finnish artist. He died four years later. She lives in Fehmarn.
> (He leans forward, intently)
> My boy, you really should talk to her. And others…Let me see—Lina Manninen—
> (his eyes light up)
> —and Christa. Christa Shroeder.

Frank begins taking notes, writing the names down as fast as Wolff can rattle them off.

> **WOLFF**
> Christa Schroeder was very close to the Führer. Use my name. She was one of his secretaries. Henrietta von Schirach will see you, I'm sure. I will send you the information on how to reach them.
> (his eyes narrow, thinking)
> Medard Klapper is very active, I hear but, no—
> (a dismissive wave of his hand)
> —no, forget Klapper. Let's see. There are so few…and yet so

> many. Ah, Dr. Hottl! And Hermann Giesler…I will contact them for you…

WAGNER swells, masking the sound of the door as it opens behind them. But Wolff, used to years of being on guard, stops talking and turns to see—

Wilhelm standing in the room, like an errand boy waiting for a tip. Frank stands politely.

> FRANK
> General Wolff, my grandfather, Wilhelm Brandenburg.

Wolff rises and clasps the older man's hand in his.

> WOLFF
> (effusive, warm)
> An honor, sir. An honor to meet you. Were you with the Reich? Please…
> (motions to chair)
> …join us. We are reminiscing.

Wilhelm casts a glance at Frank who nods his assent. He sits, tentatively, in awe that General Karl Wolff—the man he heard about his whole life, whose name was so much a part of his youth—is here in his fruit cellar, talking to his grandson.

> FRANK
> Would you like a glass of wine, Opa?

> WILHELM
> Yes, thank you, Frank.

Wolff studies Wilhelm while Frank pours the wine, hands it to his grandfather, and then resets the Wagner tape.

> WOLFF
> So. Where did you serve? You should be very proud of your grandson.

> WILHELM
> In the NSKK. Here in Hildesheim. Not at your level, I assure you. But I have heard much of you—my whole life. It is very kind of you to—
> (gropes for the right word)
> —"mentor" my grandson.

An especially LUSH refrain of Wagner plays. Wolff closes his eyes and takes a deep breath, as if inhaling the sound. After a moment he opens his eyes and replies to Wilhelm.

The Brandenburg Quest

                                WOLFF
            It is *my* honor. My memories will die unless I share them with
            youth.
                         (motions around room)
            These…are my memories…
                         (holds out his hand for both to see)
            And *this*—

70   CLOSE ON—WOLFF'S HAND and a GOLD SIGNET RING on his finger.

                                WOLFF (O.C.)
            —is the signet ring of Hermann Göring! His daughter, Edda,
            gave it to me.

BACK TO SCENE

Frank and Wilhelm lean in. Their eyes widen, impressed. Wolff smiles at Frank.

                                WOLFF
            I, too, have a few mementos, although not in such a memory-
            stirring place as this.

71   CLOSE ON—HITLER POSTER ON THE WALL

BACK TO SCENE

                                WOLFF
            And how is your research going, Frank? Successfully I trust.

                                FRANK
            Yes, Herr General, thanks to you. Tomorrow I am seeing
            Generalleutnant Adolf Galland.

                                                              DISSOLVE TO:

72   INT. ADOLF GALLAND'S OFFICE—DAY

ADOLF GALLAND, 70s, sits stiffly behind his desk with a small Führer like moustache, wearing a conservative gray suit with a bright red tie.

SUPER: ADOLF GALLAND, GENERALLEUTNANT DER LUFTWAFFE

He runs a finger along the edge of a photograph Frank has brought him as a gift.

                                FRANK [WE SEE PIC.]
            I'm glad you like it, Herr Galland. I had it made especially for
            you.

Galland looks over at Frank, saying nothing, sizing him up. A heavy silence hangs between them. Finally he speaks:

GALLAND

To answer your question…yes, I knew the Führer. I also saw him at Wolfsschanze. He had his dogs with him. The Führer was very fond of dogs, you know? He had those three German shepherds, of course. What were their names again?

FRANK

Blondie!

GALLAND

Right. And Wolf. And the big black one. What was that third dog's name.

He looks at Frank closely. Frank thinks a moment, then shakes his head.

FRANK

I don't know. I don't think I ever knew.

Galland pulls back.

GALLAND

No matter…
(smiles)

An icy reserve settles in. The interview is over.

73 INT. BRANDENBURG HOUSE—LIVING ROOM

Frank holds a bouquet of flowers tied with pink ribbon in one hand, a briefcase in another, having graduated from duffel bag to briefcase. A small overnight case sits on the floor at his feet.

His father paces in front of him.

KARL-PETER

It's bad enough you put yourself at risk, but to put your family at risk, too! To bring men like Karl Wolff into this house! Have you lost your mind? We *live* here! And now—where are you going? You don't know who might be watching. The Nazis are still among us. They won't go away. They are not ordinary criminals, these men. They hide in ordinary *people*—like you and me.
(stops in front of Frank)
You want the truth? Go to Dachau. Go to Auschwitz!

The Brandenburg Quest

Frank sits down, speechless, setting his flowers aside with his briefcase. He puts his head in his hands, then looks up at his father.

>   FRANK
>   (quiet anger)
> If that is the case—if they are "criminals"—then why didn't
> you tell me? Why didn't anyone?

>   KARL-PETER
>   (firm)
> Because we want it to be over! Can't you see that? We have to
> put them in the past, and to do that…we can't talk about it!

Frank gathers his things and starts out.

>   FRANK
> Then I will!

74 EXT. HALLWAY

Frank hands the bouquet of flowers with the pink ribbon to a plump woman, CHRISTA SCHROEDER, 70s.

SUPER: CHRISTA SCHROEDER, HITLER'S SECRETARY

She smiles and takes them, motioning him in.

>   FRAU SCHROEDER
> *Bitte sehr.*

75 INT. SCHROEDER'S APARTMENT—DAY

Frank and Frau Schroeder sip coffee as Frau Schroeder talks.

>   FRAU SCHROEDER
> "You must go, Christa," the Führer said to me. "I am starting
> a resistance movement in Bavaria, and I need you there for
> that. You mean the most to me." I cried, Herr Brandenburg,
> I cried. And the Führer tried to comfort me. "We shall see
> each other soon again," he promised. "I shall be coming down
> there myself in a few days."
>   (beat)
> He never did.

>   FRANK
> But you left when he asked you to?

                    FRAU SCHROEDER
                    (nods sadly, yes)
Late in the evening of April 20th ten planes left Berlin. I was on one of them. It was General Baur's operation…The last plane carried the Führer's personal documents. Later I was told it was shot down.

Frank leans in, alerted.

                    FRANK
Documents? What documents, Fräulein Schroeder?

                    FRAU SCHROEDER
They were supposed to very important. And secret. There were many cases of them.

                    FRANK
What happened to the plane? And the documents after it was shot down?

                    FRAU SCHROEDER
No one knows, Herr Brandenburg. The plane, everyone and everything in it, was lost. And it had such a lovely name, that operation. Most of them had such…mundane names. But this one: *Geheimoperation Serail*. Secret Operation Seraglio.

                    FRANK
And it was General Baur's?

She nods yes, and gets a dreamy expression on her face.

                    FRAU SCHROEDER
Operation Seraglio.
                    (softly)
Seraglio. It was such a romantic name. A sultan's harem. It brought us visions of wafting palm fronds and the fragrance of jasmine. And protection. Not at all like the columns of black smoke and the stench of a burning Berlin, overrun with Russian barbarians. You see, *ja*?

She pours another cup of coffee.

                    FRAU SCHROEDER
The Führer was always so considerate of others. I remember once. It was my birthday and I was sick in the hospital. The Führer sent me beautiful flowers and champagne. And a note asking me to get well, written in his own hand!

FRANK
That certainly was considerate of him.

FRAU SCHROEDER
(sternly)
More than that, Herr Brandenburg. It was…an honor. You see, when the Führer was reminded—as he always was by his adjutant—of someone's birthday, anniversary, or loss, he made strict distinctions as to how his response should be handled. A brief note with only his signature and flowers chosen by his adjutant, were a mere step above a simple printed card. But if it were a special person, the Führer would write the note and select the flowers himself. So you see, his solicitude for me was in a category all its own. An honor, *ja*?

FRANK
Yes, Fräulein, I agree.

FRAU SCHROEDER
The Führer always thought of others. One of his last concerns was for his friends. That is why he took such extreme steps to protect them. At the end.

FRANK
In what way do you mean, Fräulein?

FRAU SCHROEDER
That night of April 20th those ten planes that left Berlin, the tenth plane, the one that was lost, the one that carried the most important, the most secretive of the Führer's personal papers, his most sensitive inteligence documents. The Führer himself and Schaub, his adjutant, had spent hours sorting through them and burning the less important ones. It was of the greatest importance to the Führer that they survive, and he had personally picked the pilot to fly that vital mission, a Major Gundelfinger.

FRANK
But—what were these papers? I—I don't understand.

FRAU SCHROEDER
Then listen. The Führer had a far-flung network of confidants—from all over the world. Not an ordinary network, mind you. Some didn't even know they were part of it.
(off his amazed look)
Hear me out, Herr Brandenburg. Throughout the Führer's

> rise to power he was in constant contact with many of the world's top leaders: powerful, influential men in all areas. Big business. Politics. Scientists. Many important industrialists. And he kept all their plans, confidences and advice—in those three safes. Everything!
> (a knowing smile)
> After all, the Führer could not have reached the level of his power without the help of such people—conscious or otherwise—now, could he? What was in those boxes, Herr Brandenburg, was a veritable blueprint for this successors, on how to take over the world!

Frank begins writing as fast as Frau Schroeder rattles off names, proud of her insider status with the Führer.

> FRAU SCHROEDER
> …Mussolini, Admiral Horthy, King Boris of Bulgaria, Lords Londonderry and Rothermere, the British newspaper king. The Führer wrote articles for his papers—under a pen name, of course. *Amerikaners* Joseph Kennedy, Lindbergh, Harriman. There were Indian maharajas, Chinese generals. Kings of Siam and Egypt, including Farouk, to whom the Führer gave a beautiful Mercedes. And the Shah of Persia, Reza Pahlavi, who also got a Mercedes and spent much of the war in Berlin. the Iman of Yemen, Yahya, and the Agha Kahn who—to the delight of the Führer—knew whole passages from *Mein Kampf* by heart…
> (drones on)
> Chamberlain, the Duke of Windsor. Molotov…Franco. Petain. The Führer admired Marshal Petain…

DISSOLVE TO:

A tired Frank drains the last of his coffee. Frau Schroeder is now fighting back tears.

> FRAU SCHROEDER
> (dramatically)
> "We have been cut off," he said…Your car cannot get through."
> (a pitiful sigh)
> His voice, once vigorous, was flat and dead. He told me we would have to fly out. I never heard the Führer so sad, so dull. He stopped speaking in mid-sentence; I said something to him, but he didn't answer. I never heard his voice again.

She looks at Frank. Tears fall from her eyes.

CUT TO:

76   INT. VON SCHIRACH'S APARTMENT—DAY

Frank presents a box of chocolates to HENRIETTE VON SCHIRACH, 70s, who motions him in—

SUPER: HENRIETTE VON SCHIRACH

—and leads him through her small, one-room apartment. The walls are lined with photographs: framed black-and-whites and sepias. Art. She motions to them.

> FRAU VON SCHIRACH
> (re photographs)
> My father's work. He was, you know, Hitler's personal photographer. But of course you know that. That's why you're here.

She leads him out to her terrace, ringed with planter boxes overgrown with knotgrass. She stands, waist-deep among her plants, like an exotic bird in a lilac pullover, black pants and black boots.

DISSOLVE TO:

Frau Von Schirach, lucid but unsteady, has fortified herself for the meeting by tippling. She looks into the CAMERA.

> FRAU VON SCHIRACH
> Oh, I'm certain he knew. How could he not.

> FRANK
> What makes you think so?

> FRAU VON SCHIRACH
> In the spring of 1943, I was visiting friends in Amsterdam. One night in my hotel, I was aroused from my sleep by the screams and cries of women in the street below. I looked out the window and saw a large group—women of all ages—being herded, brutally, into trucks by German soldiers. The next morning no one in the hotel would discuss it with me. But my friends told me the women were Jewesses being rounded up for transport to the camps abroad. I was deeply shaken. These women were obviously being mistreated, and I vowed to tell the Führer about it at the first opportunity. Shortly afterwards, my husband and I were invited to Berchtesgaden. After dinner I told Hitler what I had seen.
> (stops a moment and savors the memory)

There was an uneasy silence. No one spoke a word. Hitler was visibly shaken. Finally he turned on me with such venom. "What concern of yours are the Jewesses in Holland?" Then he launched into a nasty speech. To me. "Do you not understand," he said, "everyday ten thousand of my men die, irreplaceable men.

The best. The balance no longer adds up. The parity of strength…"—or words to that effect—"…in Europe will no longer exist if the *others* do not cease to be. If they live, those in the camps, those inferiors, how will it be in Europe in a hundred years? In a thousand? I am accountable to my people. To no one else. If I am branded a bloodhound in the eyes of the world, so be it. I care nothing about posthumous fame." Then he fixed his burning eyes on me: "You must learn to hate!" he blazed. "*I* had to."

(beat)

We were asked to leave the next day. We were never asked back.

77   INT/EXT. CAR (MOVING)—ISLE OF FEHMARN—DAY

The day is raw and overcast as Frank crosses the bridge from Travemunde to the island of Fehmarn in the Baltic Sea, east of Kiel. A dreary, monotonous landscape passes by outside the window. Frank recalls Wolff's words as he drives.

WOLFF (V.O.)
(in Frank's mind, remembering)
…at his funeral, Hitler himself eulogized Reinhard Heydrich, calling him "the man with the iron heart whose name will resound with the greatest of heroes."

FRANK (V.O.)
(to himself)
The one they called the Blond Beast. *Der Henker*—the Hangman. Most beautiful of all the Nazis. Aryan poster boy…

FRANK
(to himself)
What will *she* be like?

BACK TO:

78   INT/EXT. CAR (MOVING)—ISLE OF FEHMARN—LATE DAY

The rain is coming down hard now as Frank drives a deserted unfamiliar country road. The sky has turned a leaden gray. It is growing dark.

The Brandenburg Quest

79 EXT. ISLE OF FEHMARN—TODENDORF—HOUSE—NIGHT

Frank pulls up in front of a modest one-story house and gets out. A cold rain pelts him and gusts of wind tear at the tree branches and rattle the peeling shutters on the house, banging them against the walls.

The house is dark, run-down, unkempt. Frank shivers and wraps his coat tight against the rain. He clutches his briefcase close. A single, feeble light illuminates the front porch as he rings the bell.

The old woman who opens the door looks like a classic WITCH.

SUPER: LINA VON OSTEN HEYDRICH MANNINEN

She is "LINA HEYDRICH," the once-beautiful widow of one of the Third Reich's most dashing and powerful men.

> FRANK
> Frau Heydrich—uh, Frau Manninen?

She nods her ravaged head, dislodging a few gray strands of hair which fall over her eyes, then brushes them away with impatient gestures. She motions him in.

> FRAU MANNINEN
> *Bitte*. I want to close the door against the rain.

80 INT. LINA HEYDRICH'S HOUSE—CONTINUOUS

Franks follows as she shuffles into the dimly lit house on ragged slippers that whisper across the bare floors. She wears a soiled white nightgown with a high neck and frayed lace. She motions to a thread-bare easy chair.

> FRAU MANNINEN
> *Bitte*. Please sit.

Frank does, and looks around. A MASK of Heydrich's perfect face is mounted on one wall along with a dreamy photograph of Lina, Reinhard, their son and two daughters, and a large color print of a three-masted schooner.

Lina sits down on a sagging sofa; cocking her head, she peers at Frank with rheumy eyes.

> FRAU MANNINEN
> Why are you here, Herr Brandenburg?

> FRANK
> I wanted to meet you, Frau Heydrich. I know so much about
> your husband, and I wanted to meet you.
> (off her stare)

                    I wanted to talk with you. About your husband, perhaps.

He opens his briefcase and takes out several photos he has made, handing them to her.

                              FRANK
          And to give you these…as an inadequate little gift, which I beg you to accept.

She looks at the photographs, holding the portrait of Reinhard in front of her. Her eyes brim as she stares at it.

                         FRAU MANNINEN
                    It is a very good picture of my husband. It was very good of
                    you to bring it.

81   CLOSE SHOT—B&W PHOTOGRAPH

It shows a handsome young Reinhard Heydrich at a ball, dancing with a lovely young girl, Lina von Osten.

[BACK TO SCENE]

Now tears run freely down her sunken cheeks and her voice wavers.

                         FRAU MANNINEN
                    Oh, if my Reinhard could only have been alive to see you
                    come here. With this picture. To talk about him. He would
                    have been so pleased.

She wipes the tears from her eyes with her sleeve and clutches the photograph to her bosom, then looks at Frank.

                         FRAU MANNINEN
                    What do you want to know? What can I tell you?

                                                                              DISSOLVE TO:

                              FRANK
                    In the film, they show your husband involved in what they
                    call the Final Solution. What can you tell me about that?

                         FRAU MANNINEN
                    You mean the extermination of the Jews. I know what the
                    Americans, and the British, say about Reinhard. But it is not
                    true! Reinhard had nothing to do with all that. I would have
                    known. He had more important things to do.
                              (growing angry)

Most of what is written and said about my husband is deceitful and distorted to conform to what is—required by the views of the time. And such views change with the times. It is so easy to do. If something bothers your precious conscience, blame it on someone else. Someone who cannot defend himself. Someone—dead. That is what Germany is doing today.
> (her anger gives way to tears)

They have all been so unfair to Reinhard. There was no reason that Swiss diplomat called my husband "The God of Death." It was just for effect. Politics.
> (beat)

The Jews, they caused us so much grief. So much trouble. But Reinhard had nothing to do with your—your 'Holocaust.' He was a victim, like them. Assassinated.

FRANK

I know.

FRAU MANNINEN

No. Not by the grenade. By Hitler. The Führer thought Reinhardt was getting too popular. He was jealous. He felt—threatened.
> (off Frank's startled look)

My Reinhardt was in the hospital, recovering. He was doing very well, almost back to his old self…Then the Führer sent his personal physician to take care of Reinhardt…Four days later he was dead. DEAD. Herr Brandenburg. You can ask General Wolff—he knows.
> (nods to wall)

That is his death mask. It is bronze. It was an S3 ritual to make such a mask. You must look at it more closely. It is beautiful.

She rises and turns on a lamp. A RED LIGHT bathes the room in crimson. The mask on the wall glows, dark red. Frank crosses to inspect it.

82   CLOSE ON—DEATH MASK

The only sounds in the room are the driving rain outside, the howling wind and the scratching of the bare limbs of trees against the house.

BACK TO SCENE

FRAU MANNINEN

The man who was sent to Prague to catch Reinhard's so-called assassins, said that his death mask showed…spiritual-

ity and beauty. Like a cardinal of the Renaissance.
>> (turns back to Frank)
Could such a man have done all the things they say he did?

She smiles. A sad and toothless smile.

>> FRAU MANNINEN
> But the Jews. Today they are everywhere. Again.
>> (sighs)
> I remember once in Munich, fifty years ago. Reinhard had been appointed commissioner of police—of the SA. But the SS had all the fun.
>> (smiles at the memory)
> They were supposed to arrest enemies and they caught up with the Jew, Levy, leader of the Jews in Munich. They chased him through the streets with dog whips, and they took his shoes and socks away from him and he had to run barefoot all the way home so they could get his things.
>> (peers at Frank)
> But no one really harmed him.

She chuckles at the happy memories as she returns to the sofa and sits back down.

>> FRAU MANNINEN
> They used to sing a little ditty in those days…
>> (cackled singing)
> "Swastika on helmet. Black-white-red armband. Storm Division Hitler, we're known throughout the land!"
>> (regards Frank, tears in her eyes)
> Those were happier days, young man. So many friends.

>> FRANK
> After the war, many of your friends were successful in escaping from the Allies—Adolf Eichmann, Barbie, Müller and Mengele—
>> (and now for the 64 dollar question)
> What about Bormann? Martin Bormann. Do you think he, too, got out?

Frau Manninen shrugs.

>> FRAU MANNINEN
> I have no personal knowledge of that, Herr Brandenburg, but Bormann was a survivor. If *anyone* could get out—it would be Martin Bormann…

It is obvious that she deliberately is changing the subject.

> FRAU MANNINEN
> There is something else I want you see.

She shuffles over to a big chest and opens it. Carefully she brings out an SS Officer's tunic. Cradling it as if it were a baby, she carries it over to Frank. Frank stares at it.

83 CLOSE SHOT—TUNIC

Its once-gleaming silver insignia are dull and tarnished. The black cloth has several jagged holes in it, and dark stains that look deep blood-red in the crimson light from the lightbulb in the room.

[BACK TO SCENE]

> FRAU MANNINEN
> He wore it that day!
> (It sounds like a prayer)
> You may touch it.

Frank really does not want to do it, but he touches the stained cloth briefly. He MUST change the subject.

> FRANK
> How—how did you meet your husband, Frau Manninen?

Frau Manninen lightens up. As she is putting away the tunic—

> FRAU MANNINEN
> I met him at a dance. There were mostly girls there, and I was just about to leave when this tall, handsome Navy officer came up to me and asked me to dance. It was Reinhard. He took me home, and I was never the same again. Within a few days, he proposed. A few days, Herr Brandenburg!

She rises and crosses to the desk where she picks up an ornate porcelain CANDLESTICK.

> FRAU MANNINEN
> He gave me this as a wedding gift. It is a *Julleuchter*. It was presented to him by the SS on some special occasion.
> (impulsively, holding it out)
> Here. I want you to have it.

> FRANK
> Oh, no, Frau Heydrich. I couldn't. Your son. Your daughters…

                    FRAU MANNINEN
                  (shaking her head firmly)
         No. I want you to have it. I shall not be around much longer,
         and I know you will keep it safe and give it the place it de-
         serves.

                         FRANK
                      (accepting it)
              Thank you, Frau Heydrich, I am honored.

The wind howls louder. Dogs BARK outside.

                    FRAU MANNINEN
              The weather on the island can be harsh.

She pulls a tattered blanket around her shoulders.

                    FRAU MANNINEN
         But on his deathbed Reinhard said to me, "Return to Fehm-
         arn." They were his last words to me: "Return to Fehmarn."
         And I am here.

84   INT/EXT. CAR (MOVING)—ISLE OF FEHMARN—NIGHT

The windshield wipers slap across the glass to clear the rain.

Brahms' *ERNESTE GESÄNGE* plays—ON THE CAR RADIO—as Frank keeps his eyes on the road ahead, the darkness illuminated only by a circle of light from the headlights of his car. Along with the MUSIC Frank imagines:

IMAGES of a young LINA VON OSTEN dancing with the man with the iron heart: the BLOND BEAST with the perfect face.

The shot swims into the bloody tunic of Reinhard Heydrich and turn into a car blowing up, in turn into the blood red death mask of Heydrich, and a doctor giving him a shot as he lies in hospital bed...

                    FRAU MANNINEN (O.S.)
              If anyone could get out—it would be Martin Bormann...

85   INT. BRANDENBURG HOUSE—FRANK'S BUNKER

                                                          DISSOLVE TO:

CLOSE SHOT—JULLEUCHTER

CAMERA ZOOMS OUT TO WIDER SHOT TO INCLUDE FRANK

Frank rifles through his paperwork, searching files, books, throwing things into the middle of the room. In one, he finds what he's looking for. Wilhelm pokes his head though the crack in the door which Frank left open in his haste.

> FRANK
>
> I knew it! I knew it!

> WILHELM
>
> What is all the commotion, *mein Junge*?

He steps in. Frank is examining a map.

> FRANK
>
> Opa—I think that plane, the tenth plane, crashed here—
> > (he points to map)
>
> In Börnersdorf, near the Czechoslovakian Border, in the DDR, *not* in Bavaria, as history tells us.

> WILHELM
> > (motioning to the mess)
>
> Ach! I thought you might have found Martin Bormann in there.

> FRANK
> > (points to passages in two books)
>
> Look, here it is. Trevor-Roper says it was shot down in the early morning hours of April twenty-first; O'Donnell says it crashed later—in Bavaria.

He grabs a paper off his desk and holds it out.

> FRANK
> > (offering it)
>
> But look at this.

Wilhelm takes it and begins reading:

> WILHELM
>
> "The Agency for Notification of Nearest Relatives of Fallen Former Members of the…

Impatient, Frank grabs it and reads aloud the important parts.

> FRANK
>
> "We regret to inform you we cannot give you the information…" No—
> > (skipping down)
>
> —here.

                    (reading)
"Major Friedrich Gundelfinger, born May nineteenth 1900 in Munich. Fallen April twenty-first, 1945, six A.M., near Börnersdorf, Dippoldswalde. Buried: Börnersdorf Cemetery." Gundelfinger was the pilot of that tenth plane, with Hitler's personal papers.

                    WILHELM
How do you know that?

                    FRANK
Frau Schroeder told me.

                    WILHELM
How would she know?

                    FRANK
Opa! She was Hitler's PERSONAL secretary! Hitler's secret documents were on that plane.

Wilhelm hesitates, then turns dismissively.

                    WILHELM
Recipes for strudel, no doubt.

                    FRANK
Opa…his plan to set up a new world order for the Nazis. A Fourth Reich!

Wilhelm shakes his head and starts out, then turns:

                    WILHELM
He was a madman, Frank. Madmen don't set up worlds—much less Orders.

                    FRANK
Baur told me that the Führer had given Bormann some special orders—a special mission. He didn't know what. Opa, perhaps those orders were in the papers. Perhaps there is a clue to where Bormann might be?

                                                DISSOLVE TO:

86 INT. BAUR'S VILLA—LIVING ROOM—DAY

Frank watches Baur waiting for an answer. After a moment of silence, Baur sighs.

BAUR

Seraglio? Of course I remember it. I wish you had not asked me about Operation Serail.

FRANK

Herr General, I—I'm sorry, I did not—

Baur holds up a hand to silence him.

BAUR

You could not have known, my boy. But Serail is a—a very painful memory for me. I have been asked about it before. I have always refused any comment.
    (silence for a moment, then he looks up)
Frank, I shall tell you about Secret Operation Seraglio.

Frau Baur enters with a vase of freshly arranged flowers and smiles at Frank.

FRAU BAUR
(to Frank)

So kind of you.
    (to Baur)
Aren't they lovely, Hans?

She sets them down and fusses with the arrangement while Baur talks.

BAUR

The first plane took off from Gatow April 20 shortly after twenty-one hundred hours. Eight more departed the following hour, till midnight. Christa Schroeder, who you talked to, was on one of those planes. All nine arrived safely and on schedule at Munich and Salzburg.
    (sighs)
The tenth plane, a JU-352, had engine trouble. Its departure was delayed until the early hours of the twenty-first. The documents were aboard that plane. I was not informed of what they were, but they were sealed in heavy crates: ten or more.
    (looks at Frank bleakly)
That plane, my boy, never did arrive. I had to tell *unser Vati* it was lost, that my Operation Seraglio was a failure. He was shaken, Frank. He took it hard. He had tears in his eyes. "It had to be the plane with the crates," he said bitterly, "With the documents that would have been so important for the world of the future."
    (a beat)
He cried, my boy, he cried.

                              FRANK
Was the plane, or the wreck, ever found?

                              BAUR
                       (shakes his head)
There was talk of some Bavarian farmers who heard it crash.
They investigated some time after the war but found no eye-
witnesses, no wreck, no documents.

                              FRANK
You're sure it was Bavaria?

                              BAUR
I should know. It was my failure. My plane—shot down or
crashed. Destroyed anyhow.
                           (beat)
It has taken me many years to live with my…betrayal. And
betrayal it was. I had assured *unser Vati* I could fly him out—
anywhere; it was as good as a lie. If the pilot of that ill-fated
plane could not avoid disaster, neither could I. Gundelfinger
was a first-rate pilot.

Frank sits up at the name.

                              FRANK
So…the pilot of this plane was Gundelfinger?

                              BAUR
                       (nods, remembering)
Major Friedrich Gundelfinger.

Frank smiles, grateful to Baur for confirming this clue in his on-going scavenger hunt.

                              FRANK
Thank you, Herr General.

87   EXT. PRIEN AM CHIEMSEE—KIRCHENWEG—ZIEGGMAN HOUSE—DAY

Frank knocks on the door of a white, two-story house with brown shutters, a big garden
and a fish pond with goldfish.

88   INT. ZIEGGMAN HOUSE—LIVING ROOM—DAY

Frank is seated by a roaring fire when Wolff reenters the living room with a slip of paper.
He hands it to Frank as he sits.

                        WOLFF
            Here it is. "Wil-helm Hot-tl"…He may or may not meet with
            you.

                        FRANK
            Thank you, Herr General.
                    (glances at slip)
            I do not know of this Dr. Hottl.

                        WOLFF
            Of course, you would not. He was not a big fish.

                        FRANK
            Who is he, then?

                        WOLFF
            Was. It's who he was. SS—Obersturmbannführer Hottl served
            under…Schellenberg.

                        FRANK
            Schellenberg?! Head of foreign espionage for the Reich?

Wolff nods.

                        FRANK
            When I call on him, Herr General—and the others—may I be
            allowed to use your name?

Wolff contemplates Frank a beat, steeples his hands—as if in prayer—and closes his eyes, reflecting, then speaks.

                        WOLFF
            I believe—I believe you *are* seriously interested in the old
            days, Frank. I believe you do want to find out the truth of
            matters as they were—and as they are. I think it's about time I
            did something about it.

                        FRANK
                    (puzzled)
            What, Herr General?

Slowly Wolff reaches into his pocket, pulls out something, and holds it out to Frank.

                        WOLFF
            This.

89   CLOSE ON—WOLFF'S RING

                             WOLFF

     I want you to have it.

Frank looks at it, speechless, overcome by Wolff's gesture. Finally he manages to speak.

                             FRANK

     Thank you, Herr General…I—I shall treasure it.

                             WOLFF

     And find good use for it, I trust. Of course it does not guarantee
     cooperation. Those days are gone. But it may open wider a door
     or two that otherwise might only be opened a crack, or not at all.
                         (smiles)
     A little "Open Sesame," if you will.
                         (suddenly serious)
     Carry it with you, my boy. But…do not wear it.

90   INT. BRANDENBURG HOUSE—FRANK'S BUNKER

Frank is sorting through index cards, organizing them alphabetically. He pulls one out.

                             FRANK

     Klapper…

Not interested. He sets it aside and pulls out several more.

                             FRANK

     Jordan, Giesler…
                         (setting them aside)
     Hottl…
                         (holds it up)
     This one.

A beat. He looks through his massive collection of index cards—old Nazi names and ties—then shakes his head.

                             FRANK

     So many…

He finds a card and studies it, then reaches for the phone. He dials a number—a very long number, clearly overseas—and waits while it rings, somewhat startled when it answers.

                             FRANK
                         (formal, into phone)
     Good…morning. I am calling from Germany. I am trying to
     reach a Dr. Robert Kempner. The Chief American Prosecutor
     at Nürnberg.

>   (listens)
> Ah, good. Let me explain. I am a German student studying
> the holocaust. I understand Dr. Kempner is a very busy man
> but I was wondering if—
>   (listens a beat)
> An office in Königstein. Very good. And he's in Germany when?
>   (writes down a date)
> I'm in Hildesheim. I could meet him—
>   (interrupted, a beat)
> I understand that but, please, let me explain…

91   EXT. KÖNIGSTEIN—HOTEL SONNENHOF—DAY

Dressed in his Sunday best, polished and spit-shined, Frank arrives at the former Rothschild palace.

92   INT. LOBBY—HOTEL SONNENHOF—DAY

Frank makes his way past potted palms in the lobby of the former hotel. In a secluded corner, he finds ROBERT KEMPNER, a delicate man with pure white hair and moustache.

SUPER: ROBERT KEMPNER, U.S. CHIEF PROSECUTOR AT THE NÜRNBERG TRIALS

Kempner greets Frank with old-world courtesy and introduces his two SECRETARIES.

>   KEMPNER
>   (re women)
> Miss Lester and Miss Lipton were with me at Nürnberg.

Kempner motions for Frank and the women to sit. He remains standing, occasionally pacing, firing questions at Frank, ever the prosecutor. His secretaries take notes.

>   KEMPNER
> What do you want from me? Why are you doing this? What
> are your reasons? And…when?

>   FRANK
>   (taken aback)
> When?

>   KEMPNER
> Yes…when? I presume you have other things to do with your
> life than talk to Nazi war criminals.

>   FRANK
> Yes, sir, I'm a student. In Lübeck. I do this weekends, vacations, any free time I have.

Kempner gives a little snort—of disbelief or disdain.

> KEMPNER
> And how do you pay for all this? Your father's money?

> FRANK
> Actually, sir…they're paying for it themselves.
> (smug smile)
> I've been collecting their autographs. For friends, I tell them.

> KEMPNER
> And whom have you seen?

Frank rattles off names. Again, they come easily to him.

> FRANK
> Hans Baur, Oberstgruppenführer Karl Wolff, Ministerialdirigent Heinrich Heim, the Luftwaffe ace, Oberst Hans Ulrich Rudel—

> KEMPNER
> (cutting him off)
> These men are murderers! You realize that?

Frank is speechless.

> KEMPNER
> Do you…admire…any of them?

A beat. Frank answers honestly

> FRANK
> In some cases, yes. In some ways. Rudel has shown great courage. And many of them were ignorant—

> KEMPNER
> (cutting him off)
> Ignorant! Ha!

He stops in front of Frank, fixing him with the stare of a master-inquisitor, pinning him like a bug against the back of his gilt brocade chair.

> FRANK
> I do not admire or condone what they stand for. I am often repelled by it. But I do know what they did—and why they did it.

The Brandenburg Quest

                    KEMPNER
And you think that makes it all right to hobnob with criminals and murderers?

                    FRANK
I "hobnob" to learn, Dr. Kempner. The search for knowledge
should not be limited to hobnobbing with only the best people.

He grabs his briefcase and prepares to stand when he notices a slight smile forming on Kempner's lips.

                    KEMPNER
That is what you think, is it, young man?

                    FRANK
Yes, sir, that is exactly what I think.
                         (rises)

                    KEMPNER
                  (to his secretaries)
I like this young man. He has handled my goading well. What
do you say we help him out?

Frank sits back down, quickly. The two secretaries—all smiles—murmur their assent.

                    KEMPNER
Very well…you have got yourself an advisor. If not as a jurist,
then as a friend. A silent partner. Very silent. I shall try to shed
light on your questions, but I will not tell you what to do…nor
will I provide you with names. There you are on your own.

                                                    DISSOLVE TO:

Kempner and Frank confer over coffee and cake.

                    KEMPNER
Karl Wolff…Do you find *him* sympathetic?

                    FRANK
                  (nodding honestly)
I do. He cooperated with the Allies to end the war in Italy.
And he was a witness at Nürnberg—not one of the accused.

                    KEMPNER
                  (matter-of-factly)
He turned state's evidence, that's what he did.
                         (beat)

> You came to me for guidance. Let me give you some now.
> (beat)
> When you deal with these people—Baur, Rudel, Wolff, do not lose your perspective. Be an observer. Learn. But do not get involved. Do not forge ties that you may not be able to break. Stand apart and watch—and even that is not without danger.
> (beat)
> The bond that happens between victims and victimizers, happens between reporters and subjects as well. Karl Wolff, for instance. He did a good job of befriending you. But…do you really know the man? Do you know his involvement in the abysmal crimes of the Reich? Other than "carrying out orders," of course?

He turns to his secretary.

> KEMPNER (CONT'D)
> Jane, let me have those letters we copied for Herr Brandenburg.

Frank's mind races, remembering the many times he's heard that phrase, "carrying out orders."

The secretary picks up a battered briefcase and opens it.

> KEMPNER
> When you told my secretary in Washington you are seeing former Oberstgruppenführer Karl Wolff, I had her photocopy these letters—from the Nürnberg Trials.
> (he takes the letters from Jane)
> On the witness stand, your friend declared he had known nothing about the "terrible extermination of the Jews" as he put it. To every question about Auschwitz, Lublin, Treblinka…he knew nothing. I'm certain he has told you that, too.
> (a deep sigh)
> I have heard "*I knew nothing about those camps until after the war,*" at least a thousand times. And I am sure you have too.

Frank nods, trying to collect his thoughts. Kempner has hit a nerve. He hands Frank a page.

> KEMPNER
> (re first letter)
> July 28, 1942. *1942*! It's to Wolff from the acting director of the Reich Railroads, a man named Ganzenmüller. This—
> (hands him the other letter)

                    —is Wolff's reply. August 13, 1942. Please read them.

Frank scans the first letter, then the second one—from General Wolff. The blood drains from his face.

>   WOLFF (V.O.)
>   It is with special pleasure that I take note of your information
>   that, beginning already fourteen days ago, daily trains each
>   with five thousand members of the chosen people are depart-
>   ing for Treblinka, so that we in that way are able to expedite
>   the flow of that segment of the populace at accelerated pace."

Frank stares at the letter, remembering Wolff's words to him.

>   WOLFF (V.O.)
>   *Personally I had nothing to do with those concentration camps.
>   My duties included many things, but never that! The evidence
>   against me was lies. Lies made up by the international Jews…*
>   (the letter)
>   *…trains each with five thousand members of the chosen peo-
>   ple…to expedite the flow…*

Frank slumps in his seat, shaken, betrayed. Without a word, he hands the two letters back to Kempner. Their eyes lock.

93   EXT. HAUPTSTAATSARCHIV NÜRNBERG—DAY

Frank approaches the Main State Archives building in Nürnberg and walks up the steps.

>   KEMPNER (V.O.)
>   (in Frank's head)
>   I haven't heard of them, but if they were involved in any way,
>   their names will be on the records at the *Hauptstaatsarchiv
>   Nürnberg* archives. I doubt if they will let you see them.

94   INT. HAUPTSTAATSARCHIV NÜRNBERG—CONTINUOUS

Frank enters, surprised to see high windows that light the musty shelves, half-obscured by dropcloths and scaffolding.

[Obviously there is some painting going on.]

He looks around at mile-upon-mile of stacks that seem to stretch forever in the dust-beam sun that infiltrates the archives.

95   AT THE RECEPTION DESK

He waits, watching a WOMAN'S HEAD bob above a stack at the far end of the room and makes a mental note of where it is. The head dips and rises, then disappears. Soon an attractive LIBRARIAN #1 emerges from the stacks.

> LIBRARIAN #1
> I'm sorry. The files are classified.

> FRANK
> I only want to look at them here.

> LIBRARIAN #1
> That is impossible. They are marked "Secret." The Administrator is out today; and I will be out tomorrow. If you come back the following day, I will see what I can do.

> FRANK
> (nods politely)
> *Danke Schoen, Fräulein.*

He leaves.

96   INT. HAUPTSTAATSARCHIV NÜRNBERG—NEXT DAY

Frank enters dressed in a painter's uniform, a dropcloth over one arm. At the reception desk, a frumpy LIBRARIAN #2 is absorbed in her work. He breezes by her…

> FRANK
> (cheery)
> *Gruss Gott.*

She looks up, startled.

> LIBRARIAN #2
> And where do you think you're going?

> FRANK
> (points to stacks)
> Some touch up work. Back there.

> LIBRARIAN #2
> I don't think…that's a good idea.

He stops and turns to leave—it's no big deal—then turns back. A big smile.

> FRANK
> All right, no extra pay for me today, but I love you anyway.
> (winks)

He's irresistible. She blushes. A sudden change of heart.

                LIBRARIAN #2
       Wait. Will it take long?

                FRANK
       Just a few minutes for the first coat; a few minutes later on for
       the second.

                LIBRARIAN #2
       All right. Off with you, then!

He tips his soiled cap and heads for the aisle the other Librarian emerged from the day before.

97   A SERIES OF SHOTS

    A)   Frank wanders down the aisle checking the numbers with those on the crumpled piece of paper in his pocket.

    B)   Frank climbs a ladder, searches through a box, then removes a folder and wraps his dropcloth around it.

    C)   Frank nonchalantly walks by the desk.

    D)   Frank photocopies the contents from a self-service machine at a copy place down the street.

    E)   Frank takes the fresh copies, seals them in an envelope, and hands them to a girl at the counter for safe-keeping.

    F)   Frank returns to the Library.

98   INT. HAUPTSTAATSARCHIV NÜRNBERG—NEXT DAY

Frank waves cheerily and calls out to the frumpy Librarian.

                FRANK
       Should be ready for that second coat by now.

He passes by, file folder hidden in the dropcloth, whistling as he goes.

99   INT. BRANDENBURG HOUSE—FRANK'S BUNKER

Frank yawns and leans back, pushing aside the papers he's copied from the archives. It's after midnight. A new stack of index cards has formed at the corner of the desk. He closes his eyes, tired.

                WOLFF (V.O.)

> *Personally I had nothing to do with those concentration camps. My duties included many things, but never that! The evidence against me was lies. Lies made up by the international Jews...*

100   EXT. ZIEGGMAN HOUSE—DAY

Frank knocks on the door, resolved to confront Wolff's lies.

A drawn and gaunt Wolff, ill, opens the door, greeting him warmly, his illness forgotten at his joy in seeing Frank again. Frank stares at the changed man.

101   INT. ZIEGGMAN HOUSE—LIVING ROOM—DAY

Wolff, almost his old self, chats with Frank before the FIRE.

                WOLFF
Our little talks always bring back such pleasant memories. I'm glad you came.
            (reluctantly)
I've been a little under the weather. I guess you can tell.
            (dismissing it)
Nothing serious. I shall soon be eighty-four years old! Four times your age. But you have never let that come between us. What means the most to me, Frank, is that...
            (hesitates, then leans in, emotional, voice quavering)
...at my life's end, you have let me share the beginning of yours.

Frank's heart sinks and his resolve evaporates. There's no way he can confront Wolff with what he's learned now. He gulps...and smiles, a weak smile.

                WOLFF
I don't like to feel weak. Only once I felt this way. When I was a prisoner of war. It is a terrible thing to be locked up. Time drags to where a minute becomes an hour, an hour a day, a thousand days in a year...

                                            DISSOLVE TO:

Wolff is relishing every moment of this visit.

                WOLFF
I told the press years ago. Of course they got most of it wrong. It is no wonder so many of us refuse to speak with reporters.

                FRANK
I know. I've had difficulty. Albert Bormann wouldn't even speak to me on the phone and Colonel Galland would only

talk about…mundane things. The Führer's dogs! Blondie, Wolf, and that third dog—

            WOLFF
        (absentmindedly)
    Muck.

            FRANK
    Muck?
            (aback)
    Was that the third dog's name?

Wolff turns slowly towards him, his face ashen.

            WOLFF
    You did not know…
            (to himself)
    Of course not. How could you?

            FRANK
    Know what? The name of Hitler's third dog? Muck?
            (shakes his head, no)
    I never heard it. Until now.

Wolff smiles. There's no going back.

            WOLFF
    And now you know.
            (sighs heavily)
    It would be best if you did not. Perhaps I'd better tell you why. When I gave you my ring, I told you it would be an "Open Sesame" for you. "Muck" is a code word, Frank. A password that will gain you entrance into Nirvana, Olympus, Valhalla—the *sanctum sanctorum* of the brotherhood of the surviving Nazi hierarchy. It is a powerful word. A dangerous word. A word that could cost you your life.

            FRANK
    Muck?

            WOLFF
        (smiles feebly, obviously tired)
    I am being melodramatic, I know, but I want to impress on you the real danger of the knowledge you now possess. Had I not been lulled into a feeling of safety with you, my boy, I would never have divulged that name to you.

                    (a rueful smile)
I am getting old. It would never have happened a few years ago. Never...

                    FRANK
But why Muck?

                    WOLFF
When the war began to go badly for us, some of the highest-ranking men realized the day would come when, if they wanted to escape the vengeance of the victors and avoid giving up their pound of flesh, they'd have to scatter throughout the world and—go underground, as they say. The problem then became how to keep in touch without risking discovery. And keeping in touch was important.
                    (beat)
The ideals of the Führer and the Reich could not be allowed to die, my boy. Those ideals, those beliefs must be kept alive and nourished so that some day, they may burn brightly in the world once again. And the keepers of the flame would have to be those of us abroad.
                    (beat)
But, again, how to communicate in safety? Not by letter. Letters can be intercepted and read by anyone. Not by telephone or telegram. These are far from private. Codes can be broken, and, when overheard create suspicions. Communication could be done safely only by messengers. Trusted emissaries. A code would be needed for them to authenticate themselves. A special code. A key word that could be easily woven into the conversation. It was decided Hitler's third dog be given a name known only to the select few.

                    FRANK
But that was a long time ago. Don't a lot of people know that name by now?

                    WOLFF
Many more than the original few, of course. But by necessity. We are growing old and a new generation is taking our place, Frank.
                    (gives him a meaningful look)
A new generation. And they are fully as ruthless, fully as dedicated to keeping alive and to protecting what was and is the Führer's.
                    (his eyes bore into Frank)

> Make no mistake about it, my boy. The knowledge you now possess can be dangerous. Do not reveal what you have learned—but use it wisely and with care.

He leans back in his chair, his face tired and gray.

SUPER: SS-Oberstgurppenführer Karl Wolff died four months later, on 15 July 1984.

102 INT. HILDESHEIM—BRANDENBURG HOUSE—BEDROOM—NIGHT

Frank sits in his room in the dark, watching a flickering image on television.

He turns off the television and crosses to the window, sits and looks out at the stars.

> KEMPNER (V.O.)
> *The time and the people of the Third Reich are an irresistible, bottomless abyss, Frank. I still hear from the families of Nazis, prosecuted and sentenced at Nürnberg, who want to know what their fathers—or their grandfathers—were really like; they think that, since I knew them then, I must know them now.*

> FRANK (V.O.)
> *What do you tell them?*

> KEMPNER (V.O.)
> *What can I say? I tell them the truth.*

103 FRANK'S POV—THE STARS

The branches of the bare trees, outside the window, blow in the wind.

104 EXT. LICHTERSBERG—ALTAUSSEE—HOUSE—DAY

WILHELM HOTTL opens the door to Frank wearing black Lederhosen with plain suspenders, a light gray, open-necked shirt and black socks drawn up to his bare knees. Graying hair, full over the ears, and a craggy face.

SUPER: WILHELM HOTTL

105 INT. HOTTL'S HOUSE—DAY

Hottl sits in a leather-covered chair, hands folded in front of him, languidly kneading his fingers as if washing them in slow motion.

> HOTTL
> When you called on the phone, you talked about a television show you saw which claimed a total of some ten million

> people were killed by us. Systematically. This is, of course, a lie. An exaggeration.

Again, he folds his fingers and begins his slow-motion hand-washing.

> HOTTL
> You undoubtedly know Adolf Eichmann was one of my closest friends. We spent many a wonderful time together in the old days. In fact, I hid him here, in this house, in 1945 before he went to Argentina. And I warned him, when he was over there, that Israeli agents were on to him. He did not listen. But no one knew better than SS-obersturmbannführer Adolf Eichmann the correct figure of such executions. True undesirables, criminals, and other misfits were…removed.

He eyes Frank closely for a response but Frank holds his gaze, poker-faced. Satisfied, Hottl continues:

> HOTTL
> Of course, I personally knew nothing about what was going on in the so-called concentration camps. They were work camps, as far as I knew. Not until Eichmann told me did I know. Actually, his original report to Himmler stated that four million Jews had been eliminated in the camps, but the Reichsführer had said to him, "So few? It must be more." So Eichmann made a reevaluation of six million. So you see, the accusations of today are vastly exaggerated.

A moment of silence. Frank closes his eyes—his worst fears confirmed.

> HOTTL
> I am being very honest with you. You wanted to know the truth. And Bormann, you ask? The world has been told by experts that his bones were miraculously unearthed from the rubble of a shattered Berlin. It is, of course, not true. Those remains are *not* those of Martin Bormann.

> FRANK
> If Bormann is not dead, where is he?

> HOTTL
> (curtly)
> I have no contact with Reichsleiter Bormann. I am told he escaped to South America.

> FRANK
> But you have friends. Have any of them mentioned where he is?

Hottl's looks Frank up and down, his eyes narrowing.

> HOTTL
> Please be careful, Herr Brandenburg. I am willing to help you with your research because of Karl Wolff. But I must caution you to…be very careful. And not only here, with me, Herr Brandenburg. Not only here.

106   INT. BRANDENBURG HOUSE—FRANK'S BUNKER

Frank and his grandfather are going over maps of East and West Germany. Frank points to the map.

> FRANK
> The official version is it went down there. In Bavaria. But as we now know, the tenth plane went down there. In the DDR!

> WILHELM
> Even so…forty years ago? It's not still there. Unless you think the past still lives—in air.

> FRANK
> Someone might remember. Someone who was there when it happened.

> WILHELM
> And how do you think you're going to get to Börnersdorf?

> FRANK
> I'll say I'm a student. I'll visit Auschwitz. It's done all the time. A research trip. Börnersdorf is…nearby. On the way.

> WILHELM
> Börnersdorf is off the transit road. You want to spend the rest of your life in a Soviet jail?!

107   INT. BRANDENBURG HOUSE—LIVING ROOM

Frank sits with his parents and Wilhelm in the living room, his hat-in-hand pose belying his eagerness to get going.

> WILHELM
> The E-40 runs within thirty or forty kilometers of Börnersdorf…

> KARL-PETER
> (shoots him a look)
> Whose side are you on?

> (to Frank)
> Listen to this, Frank.
> (reads from guide book)
> "All intruders are considered spies and dealt with accordingly in the DDR."
> (handing it back, to Frank)
> Imprisoned. Two years is the minimum.

FRANK
My papers are in order. Everything. I am a student. On a legitimate research trip. I will be all right.

ILSE
Promise us…you won't leave the transit road.

Frank and Wilhelm exchange a quick glance. Frank rises—as does Wilhelm.

WILHELM
He'll be careful, won't you, Frank?

Frank and Wilhelm embrace. His parents rise. He embraces his mother, who affectionately smoothes back his hair.

ILSE
I know, I know…you have to see for yourself.

He hugs her—shakes hands with his father—and starts out.

108   INT/EXT. CAR (MOVING)—AUTOBAHN—DAY

Frank drives east, the early morning sun blinding his eyes.

109   EXT. CHECKPOINT—DAY

Frank pulls up and stops, handing his papers to a GUARD who takes and scrutinizes them, looking closely for problems. Frank waits…

110   INT/EXT. CAR (MOVING)—DAY

Frank travels through East Germany—a dreary ride through what has now become a concrete Third World, devoid of beauty. We hear the "World of the Future" described by "The Man from the Past"—moving forward in time.

111   EXT. AUSCHWITZ—DAY

The WORDS: ARBEIT MACHT FREI.

SUPER: "WORK MAKES YOU FREE"

Frank stands gazing up at these WORDS that are written in large letters over the main gate into Auschwitz.

SUPER: AUSCHWITCH CONCENTRATION CAMP

112   WIDER ANGLE

Black iron gates hang from massive gateposts and stand wide open between double wooden market posts, tall and painted black-and-white, barber-pole fashion.

A barrier-boom has been lowered across the roadway and a sign on top reads: "HALT. AUSWEISE VORZEIGEN."

SUPER: "STOP. SHOW PERMITS."

At the road's end, stands a wooden post with another sign: "VORSICHT. HOCHSPANNUNG LEBENSGEFAHR."

SUPER: "CAUTION. HIGH VOLTAGE. MORTAL DANGER."

A thick RED LIGHTNING BOLT is painted across it, like a slash of blood.

Frank ducks under the boom and walks down the deserted road flanked by solid, grim, two-story red-brick buildings.

SUPER: AUSCHWITZ (1985)

Frank walks the nearly deserted camp streets, rounds a corner of a barrack and stops.

At the far end of the street, between two buildings, a tall brick wall has been erected across the road. Unlike the windows in the other buildings in the camp, the windows in the two buildings flanking the street are covered with heavy wooden shutters.

Half-way down the street, on a short flight of stairs, sits a figure in BLUE, head bowed, one hand resting on a step for support.

It is SARAH. Her face is hidden from Frank, but she has a crown of short, reddish hair. In her light blue pants-suit, dotted with tiny white flowers, she is strangely out of place in the otherwise drab surroundings.

She sits absolutely motionless, frozen in time. For a while Frank watches her, then walks towards her, concerned.

                    FRANK
          Excuse me. Are you all right?

She looks up at him with the round, pleasant face of a woman in her sixties. She nods, yes.

SARAH

I was only seeking a moment of peace where there was none…so long ago.

She stands and nods towards the wall at the far end of the street.

SARAH

That is the *Todeswand*. The Wall of Death.
(facing the wall)
Tens of thousands were shot against that wall by the SS. One was my friend, Rachel.

For a long time, she gazes at the wall. Frank remains silent, not wanting to intrude. He notices a TATTOO—on the inside of her left forearm.

113   CLOSE ON—The letter "A" followed by a NUMBER.

BACK TO SCENE

SARAH
(flat, devoid of emotion)
She was a gold retriever. She retrieved the gold in the teeth of the inmates. After they had been gassed and hosed down to clean them of the feces and blood that covered them. In their death throes. Before they were drained of blood and burned. She had to pull all the teeth with gold in them, and fill her quota of buckets.

Unnerved, Frank sways, almost losing his balance.

FRANK

And…why was she shot?

SARAH

An unpardonable crime. She kept a gold crown—to barter for a slice of bread. Some of the guards could be bribed. But a Kapo saw her and turned her in.

FRANK

Kapo?

SARAH

A trustee inmate. A spy. There were such. They traded their souls for a little better treatment.

FRANK

I—I'm sorry for your friend.

The Brandenburg Quest

Frank's remark sounds inane to him, meaningless and far away as if it's coming from someone else and he isn't really there.

> SARAH
> I am not. There were worse ways to die. Much worse.
> (points to her right)
> Over there—in block eighteen you were put in a cell and left until you starved to death lying in your own waste. Or placed in a cell in total darkness with no air to slowly suffocate. In block twenty-two they had four little bunkers—ninety by ninety by ninety…
> (aside)
> Odd how I remember those numbers…
> (back to topic)
> …centimeters. You fit by curling up into a small ball and you stayed there for days until your sentence was up, even if you died. Death came easy. If you picked up an apple core discarded by a guard, or needed to relieve yourself during work hours; or you didn't work fast enough…

FLASHBACK TO:

114   MONTAGE

Beatings. Starving faces. Men and Women beyond exhaustion, trying to work.

A MAN hangs by his arms, turned backward.

> SARAH (V.O.)
> …for hours until they were forced from their sockets.

A WOMAN pries her own tooth out.

> SARAH (V.O.)
> …to trade for food. That was always punishable by death. If they were lucky, they would die like Rachel.
> (beat)
> I was a Harvester…

We see Sarah shearing the HAIR from the corpses of dead women.

> SARAH (V.O.)
> When they liberated the camp, they found fourteen pounds of human hair in sacks…It took about twenty minutes to kill everyone in the largest gas chamber. It could hold two thousand at a time. They were told, "You'll be given a shower before we show you to your quarters." It was always the same.

Men, women, children remove their clothes.

>   SARAH (V.O.)
> No one knew, until it was too late. That way there was no resistance, no panic. It was very efficient.

Corpses pile up, like cords of wood.

>   SARAH (V.O.)
> Well, not perfect, mind you. There was one small problem. The ovens could burn only three hundred and fifty a day. Two bodies per oven of the newcomers; four of the inmates. They burned quickly, and took up less room.

BACK TO SCENE

Frank stares at Sarah as if seeing her for the first time, suddenly realizing this is probably the first time she's been back.

>   FRANK
> Have you been back before. I mean, after—

>   SARAH
>   (shakes her head, no)
> I hadn't the courage to come as a…tourist. No.
>   (slowly turns; points to wooden shutters)
> Those shutters were there to keep those inside from seeing what went on at the Wall.
>   (her eyes tear)
> But we could hear. We could hear.

She holds her hand out to him.

>   SARAH
> I am Sarah. Walk with me. Be my link to today.

Frank takes her hand. Together they walk down the street, away from the Wall of Death…

Past the GUARD TOWERS, looming dead and empty.

Past the BARBED-WIRE fence, once electrified, strung on graceful swan-neck poles, all leaning in toward the camp area as if hanging their heads in shame.

Past a long, wooden, shack-like building.

>   SARAH
> This is my block. Where I stayed.

The Brandenburg Quest

They enter.

115 INT. BARRACK—CONTINUOUS

She takes Frank's arm as if seeking comfort and safety. Inside, there are row-upon-row of three-tiered bunks.

                    SARAH
          We slept four to a bunk on wooden slats meant to hold two.
          Lying on rotten, befouled straw. We could not move…
                    (points)
          Miriam died there. She was twenty-two. They had taken her
          baby when she arrived and killed it. One evening, she just
          died. She was lying next to me. She grew cold. So very cold.

116 EXT. AUSCHWITZ—STREET—CONTINUOUS

Slowly Frank and Sarah walk down the street.

                    SARAH
                (points to building)
          That was *Krankenbau*—the hospital. Mengele worked there.
          I knew a woman they used to try to find a quick and effec-
          tive way of sterilizing the undesirables. They injected a strong
          acid into her uterus. Burned it out. When they let her go, she
          killed herself.

They continue walking, down the road, towards a railroad track. Sarah points to the tracks.

                    SARAH
          There. That is where the train stopped. And right here, where
          we now stand, is where Mengele stood.

INSERT—A DARK FORM—MENGELE, pointing, now "right," now "left"—his arms like the hands of a clock on the quarter hour, precise—shouting at the arrivals as they pour from the train. But we hear Sarah's VOICE.

                    SARAH (V.O.)
                (parroting him)
          Right!—Left!—Right!—Left!

BACK TO SCENE

                    SARAH
                (points left)
          Those who were to die at once went left…
                (points right)

> ...right for those strong enough to be useful for awhile—and the twins. All the children were put to death at once except the twins. He took all the twins to *Krankenbau*.
> (points behind her)
> And there—a little group of musicians played waltzes and marches and bright popular songs to welcome the new arrivals.

117 INSERT—MUSICIANS playing SONGS and WALTZES as the new arrivals are herded out of the boxcars and families torn apart—some herded left, others right.

BACK TO SCENE

SARAH'S VOICE CAN BE HEARD OVER THE SCENE

The CHILDREN, terrified and crying, are herded together in a group, the MOTHERS in another. Suddenly a small boy, perhaps four, breaks away from his group and screaming for his mother runs toward the adult group. A woman breaks out of the group and starts to run toward the little boy. She has taken only a few steps, when she is shot by a guard. She falls to the ground, dead. The little boy reaches her and throws his little body over his dead mother, wailing in anguish. A guard picks him up and literally throws him toward the group of children. The little boy hits the ground. He does not get up.

> SARAH
> All the children were put to death at once. They were of no use. They were gassed, or killed by injections into the heart. In many cases the parents died with them. In others, the children were simply taken from them. But all of them died. All of them. Eventually, even the twins...

Frank stands gazing at the empty, unkempt platform, his mind playing tricks on him.

INSERT—SHADOWY FORMS

float before his mind's eye.

The empty platform, crammed with people—men, women, and children, young and old; suddenly the black & white photos in his books take on color, becoming flesh and blood.

> SARAH (O.C.)
> I was tattooed.

BACK TO SCENE

Frank looks over to see Sarah rubbing the TATTOO on her arm.

> SARAH
> Did you know that Auschwitz was the only extermination camp where inmates were tattooed?

He shakes his head, no. Suddenly Sarah turns and begins walking down the railroad tracks towards the brick tower and gaping archway through which the rails lead into the camp.

Frank follows her.

Frank walks up to her. Tears are now rolling down her cheeks. She weeps silently. He takes her hand and holds it, saying nothing.

118 INT/EXT. CAR (MOVING)—EAST GERMANY—DAY

Frank is barreling along on the transit highway through a notably drab Germany, its colors muted either by Communism or the memories of Auschwitz, poisoning the land.

He pulls out to pass a huge truck loaded with gravel when he feels a jolt, and his car begins to shake up and down on the road, like driving on a giant washboard. Damn. A flat tire.

119 EXT. ROADSIDE—DAY

Traffic whizzes by while Frank changes his tire with his spare. When finished, he throws it, flat as a pancake, into the truck.

> FRANK (V.O.)
> Great. No spare. Some James Bond. You think you can sneak into East Germany and find the Serail documents and you don't even have a spare!
> (gets back in car)
> Never mind all that other MI6 stuff you're supposed to be carrying…

120 INT/EXT. CAR (MOVING)—EAST GERMANY—DAY

Frank spots an off-ramp and impulsively swerves two-lanes to exit.

121 A SERIES OF SHOTS

(A) Frank stands outside a gas station in a small town, talking to a greasy MECHANIC.

(B) Frank sits in a diner across the street from the gas station, nursing a cup of coffee and going over his notes.

(C) Frank returns to the gas station to find his car on the rack, wheel off, tools and parts strewn all over the ground below.

122 INT. GARAGE—CONTINUOUS

The mechanic is wiping his hands on a greasy rag, obviously not in a hurry.

                MECHANIC

…you damaged the steering arm. Couldn't be driven the way it was.

                FRANK

It was driving just fine!

                MECHANIC
                (shrugs)

I'm trying to help you. There's an outfit in Dresden with parts. They're on the way. I told you, I'll have it today…
                (motions to diner)
The Sauerbraten is good.

123   EXT. GARAGE—LATE DAY

Frank stands beside his now repaired car and reaches into his pocket.

                MECHANIC

Westmarks only.

                FRANK

Fine. But I want a receipt.

124   INT/EXT. CAR (MOVING)—NIGHT

In the headlights, Frank sees the sign: BORNERSDORF KREIS PIRNA, BEZIRK DRESDEN.

125   EXT. BÖRNERSDORF—ROADSIDE—NIGHT

Frank pulls over, parks his car and turns off the lights. For a moment, he sits looking out.

HIS POV—The dim shapes of houses and barns, black on black, melding together in the dark. The night is partly cloudy. A waning moon provides little more light than patches of stars that occasionally shine through.

BACK TO SCENE

Frank gets out of the car, slips his camera into his pocket, and begins walking into the village along the road.

126   INT. BÖRNERSDORF—NIGHT

The road leads him into a sleeping village, quiet and hushed. In the distance, a dog BARKS. Frank remembers what his father read in the guide book:

The Brandenburg Quest

> KARL-PETER (V.O.)
> *All intruders are considered spies and dealt with accordingly in the DDR. Imprisoned.*

> EAST GERMAN (V.O.)
> (in his mind)
> *Two years is the minimum, Herr Brandenburg. Two years…*

He steps off the road and makes his way between dark, shuttered houses until—up ahead—he sees a yellow light spilling out from a partly-opened barn door. Someone in town is awake. He quickens his pace.

As he reaches the barn, he peers in and calls out.

> FRANK
> *Holla!* Is anyone here?

The light is coming from a kerosene lamp that hangs from a rusty nail on a post. He calls again. Horses, half-hidden in their stalls, stir uneasily.

127 INT. BARN—CONTINUOUS

He walks over to the light, then up to one of the stalls and leans over, peering in. A loud VOICE booms behind him.

> VOICE (O.C.)
> *Was suchen Sie hier?*

Frank whirls around to see a burly man, face grim, holding a PITCHFORK pointed firmly at him, its well-polished points glinting in the light like a bayonet. He stares, terrified, at the FARMER.

> FRANK
> I'm—I'm a student, from Hildesheim. I'm doing research. On a plane crash near Börnersdorf. Back in the war, 1945. I'm looking for anyone knows anything about it, who remembers…

The farmer slowly lowers the pitchfork.

> FARMER
> Do the authorities know you are here?

> FRANK
> Yes, I have the proper permits and travel papers.

He fumbles for them, holds them out. The farmer sets the pitchfork aside and ignores the papers.

FARMER
I was born the year after the war. I know nothing. But...
(scratches the back of his head)
Anton Rost. He was there and has talked about it. He's an old timer. Never sleeps. But I need to check on Lotte. She's about to drop her foal. Tonight. Or tomorrow.

He disappears into the stall, then emerges.

FARMER
Come. I will take you to Rost.

128 INT. FARMHOUSE

ANTON ROST, 75, a wiry man, his face furrowed from working outdoors; he lives in a modest, typical farmer's house with rough wooden furniture, bare worn floors, a black wood-burning stove and open shelves with cracked and dented cookware.

ROST
It was a long time ago. I was still a young man. And that is a long time ago!

He cackles, showing yellowed, uneven teeth.

ROST
But I do remember. I do remember. The plane crashed here—only a few miles from the village. I was the first one out there.

He stops, lost in remembering.

FRANK
And? Do you remember when it crashed?

ROST
I do. The day before my wife—God rest her soul—used the last three eggs from the water-glass barrel. It was early in the morning, the twenty-first of April, 1945. Not much to tell, I'm afraid. The plane had crashed. It was burning.

FRANK
Did anyone—or anything—survive? Did a Major Gundelfinger?

ROST
(looks at him closely)
You know about him, young man?

                    FRANK
It is because of him I am here.

                    ROST
They all died, except two, and one of those died two days later. Becker, or some name like that. The other, I myself took him home from the wreck. He was taken to the *Militärlazarett* in Bad Gottleuba.

                    FRANK
Do you remember his name?

                    ROST
A man is apt to remember the name of someone whose life he has saved, *ja*? Westermaier. Franz Westermaier. He was a tail gunner on the plane.

                    FRANK
And the plane? Did everything burn?

                    ROST
              (nods, yes)
Everything that could burn, burned. There was a lot of scrap metal lying about, of course. That was all that remained.
              (pause)
Except for the crates.

Frank tenses.

                    FRANK
Crates?

                    ROST
Yes. The tail section had broken off so it did not burn as fiercely as the rest—and a lot of wooden crates had spilled out.

                    FRANK
What became of them? The crates?

                    ROST
They had markings on them. Important markings. Clearly, they were government property. We all agreed they should not fall into Russian hands. If they got here. So we took them to the parson's house, and hid them.

FRANK

And? Are they still there?

ROST
(shakes his head, no)
For a day they were. Then a group of men came. They asked about the crates. And we gave them to them.

FRANK

Who were these men?

ROST

Soldiers. Wehrmacht, I believe. We didn't ask. One does not question authority. They knew about the crates. They described them…so we knew they were theirs. And we gave them to them…

Frank stands, checks his watch and begins pacing.

FRANK

Where did they take them?

ROST

Let me finish in my own good time. Patience, young man.
(to the farmer)
Nine o'clock, and you find him in your barn.
(to Frank)
A strange time to come calling, young man, with even stranger questions. What, where, who…when? You want to know where they took them?
(to Farmer)
Maybe he missed his plane forty years ago. Like in the *Twilight Zone*, *ja*?
(to Frank)
Have you ever seen that American TV show?

FRANK

Of course, Herr Rost. Of course. It's just—my permit expires at midnight.

ROST

Ah, very well. I will make it brief. All I know is that they loaded them onto a truck and took them away. To Dresden, I think.
(smiles)
I bet you'd rather have found a parson's house full of crates than a cemetery full of bodies, *ja*?

The Brandenburg Quest

                    (he cackles)

Frank stops in his tracks.

                    FRANK
          Bodies. What—bodies?

                    ROST
          The ones who died in the crash, young man. Most we could
          identify by their disc and serial numbers. We have a memo-
          rial plot—in our cemetery. We buried what was left of them.
          And *they* are still there.
                    (cackles again)

                    FRANK
          Herr Rost, I thank you. I must see the cemetery—tonight. If
          you can lend me a flashlight, I shall return it before I go.

Rost motions to a kerosene lamp.

                    ROST
          I can lend you that. You need not return it tonight. God will-
          ing, I shall be asleep. Just leave it on the tree in the memorial
          plot. I will get it tomorrow.

He rises and they shake hands.

                    ROST
          Take the road through town; turn right at the second side-
          road. You can't miss it.

129   EXT. BÖRNERSDORF CEMETERY—NIGHT

Frank makes his way through the tombstones until he comes to an untended plot under a forked tree. A slab of black granite with carved white lettering reads:

SUPER: ZUM GEDENKEN—IN MEMORIAM

There are sixteen names on the marker. In the center:

SUPER: FRIEDRICH GUNDELFINGER, 19.5.1900-21.4.1945

By the light of the kerosene lamp, Frank writes down the names on the marker; then he takes out his camera and sets it on a rock, using the timer to take a photo of himself by marker. He tries another, but that was the last frame. He slips the roll into his pocket and reloads the camera.

130   A SERIES OF SNAPSHOTS—FRANK standing next to the marker, his lantern held up high, like a young Diogenes in search of the Truth.

131   INT/EXT. CAR (MOVING)—HIGHWAY—NIGHT

Frank drives along a side road. Up ahead, a slight incline leads to the main road. Nervous, he turns out his lights and drives in total darkness. As he crests the hill he sees:

132   FRANK'S POV

A car with beige-and-green markings—the VOPO, the East German People's Police. Their BLUE LIGHT blinks on and moves towards him like the fin of a shark.

BACK TO SCENE

Frank stops and puts the car in park, searching for a way out, panic on his face.

> EAST GERMAN (V.O.)
> (in his mind)
> *Two years, Herr Brandenburg. Two years. Minimum.*

133   EXT. SIDE ROAD—NIGHT

On an impulse, he throws open the car door and jumps out, running…*towards* the police car, calling out:

> FRANK
> *Bitte, Bitte.* I need help. I am lost.

The police car stops and two VOPO (Volkspolizei) officers exit. They are both armed. Frank is hurrying toward them. One of the VOPO's draws his gun.

> VOPO #1
> Stop! Stay right where you are!

FRANK stops abruptly. He looks petrified.

> VOPO #1
> Keep your hands where I can see them.

FRANK at once obeys, holding his arms along his sides away from his body. VOPO #1 walks up to Frank, while VOPO #2 covers them from a short distance.

> VOPO #1
> Papers!

FRANK fishes his papers from his pocket and hands them to the officer, knowing they are not valid papers.

FRANK

           Please, Officer—I—

                          VOPO #1

           Shut up!

FRANK falls silent.

                          VOPO #1
                          (ominously)
           You are a long way from the transit highway, Herr Branden-
           burg. You are in a zone where it is illegal for you to be. You
           are under arrest!

                          FRANK
                          (desperately)
           But officer. I—I can explain. I had a flat on the highway. Just
           below Dresden. And then—something went wrong with the
           car. I had to have it fixed.
                          (He brightens)
            Wait! I have the receipt—

He starts toward his car.

                          VOPO #1

           Stay away from the car!

FRANK stops dead in his tracks. VOPO #1 nods at VOPO #2, who at once goes to Frank's car, and rummages through the glove compartment; he finds a paper and brings it to VOPO #1, during—

                          FRANK

           I—I could not drive on without getting it fixed. Don't you
           see? I found a little gas station, just off the transit highway,
           and I took it there. It—it took hours to fix.

He points to the paper in the VOPO's hand.

           Look at the date! And the place. That's the receipt!

VOPO #1 nods to VOPO #2 who goes to the police car and gets on the radio.

                          FRANK

           Trying to get back on the transit, I got lost. It was late and I
           was very tired. Too tired to drive safely. So I—I drove off the
           road to take a nap. I just woke up, when—I was so glad to see
           you. I knew I could ask you for help.

VOPO #2 joins them, he hands Frank the receipt.

> VOPO #2
> Shurig remembers him. He had something to eat across the street.
> (he winks at Frank)
> That Saurbraten is something else, *Ja!*

> VOPO #1
> Check out his car.

VOPO #2 Goes through Frank's car. He finds his camera, opens it up and pulls out the film, throwing the camera back into the car, during—

> VOPO #1
> I would advise you, Herr Brandenburg, to be more cautious how you deport yourself while in the DDR. Not every law enforcement officer is as lenient as we are.

> FRANK
> (fervently)
> I certainly will.

> VOPO #1
> You are about seven kilometers from a transit highway on-ramp. Follow us. We will take you there.

134   INT. BRANDENBURG GREENHOUSE—DAY

The place is a sea of color; the splendor of blooms of every kind vie with each other; it is a scene of beauty—in stark contrast to the ensuing dialogue.

FRANK and KARL-PETER are tending the flowers.

> KARL-PETER
> I am pleased. They are all doing well, don't you think?

> FRANK
> (absentmindedly)
> Yes—they are…Dad, there is something I want you to know.

> KARL-PETER
> Yes?

> FRANK
> Those—those horrible things they showed in that American film, the Holocaust, they did happen. Just as they said. Only—worse. I found out.

                    KARL-PETER

Good. Now you can stop flitting around the countryside talking with war criminals. Your—your *quest* is finally over.

                    FRANK

No Dad—not just yet.

                    KARL-PETER

Now what?

                    FRANK

Bormann. Martin Bormann. Did he survive?

                    KARL-PETER

What difference does it make? Now?

                    FRANK

I must find out. I must know.

                    KARL-PETER

Why, *um Gottes Willen?*

                    FRANK

Because—if he did—it could—it might influence the future…

                    KARL-PETER

So what if you do find out that Bormann survived, what good would it do?

                    FRANK

Dad, I've heard it said that knowledge is the first step toward action. If they know the truth, they may be able to—to do the right thing.

135   EXT/INT. CAR (MOVING)—DAY

SUNLIGHT, FLASHING. Frank pulls the visor down to shade his eyes. Beside him, the seatbelt straps a POTTED PLANT into the passenger seat. It waves gently in the wind.

IN HIS MIND, we hear:

                    WOMAN'S VOICE (V.O.)

I—I cannot see you.

                    FRANK (V.O.)

Frau Westermaier, please, I realize your husband passed away three years ago, but there are relatives of others on that plane.

> Can you help me?

He hits a bump in the road and reaches over to steady the plant.

> WOMAN'S VOICE (V.O.)
> Yes...he *was* the tail gunner. But they were not shot down. They were late getting off and had to fly low since they had lost the cover of darkness. It could have been engine trouble, or low clouds. The tip of the wing clipped the top of a tall fir—and they crashed. A farmer saved him. He was taken to a local hospital. The crates were saved, but we never knew what happened to them...

136   INT. ROSENHOFF RETIREMENT HOTEL—APARTMENT—DAY

FRAU BEST sits stiffly, barely visible behind the potted plant. She nods politely to Frank with a wan smile.

> FRAU BEST
> *Danke.*

WERNER BEST, 74, in open-necked shirt and loose slacks, leans back in a comfortable chair. His pate, nearly bald, glistens in the light coming in from the window behind him. A short, unimposing man, he nurses a beer.

SUPER: WERNER BEST, FORMER REICH PLENIPOTENTIARY COMMISSIONER FOR OCCUPIED DENMARK AND SS-OBERGRUPPENFÜHRER

> BEST
> ...I can tell you I consented only because of the recommendation of Karl Wolff. Always a dear friend of mine. Otherwise, I see no one. I have had threats against my life. I also get requests from journalists and historians. I refuse them all.
>   (his eyes light on Frank, curiously penetrating)
> What do *you* want with me? What do *you* want to discuss? My reprehensible Gestapo days? My unsavory actions in Denmark?

Best speaks with a suspicious, barely concealed bitterness. Frank sets his beer aside—he doesn't drink—and dismisses all with a wave of his hand.

> FRANK
> Nothing like that, I can assure you, Herr Doktor. Enough has been written on that. I came because I wanted to talk to you, that's all.

BEST
Not out to scoop the world with some new heinous revelation?
(sardonic smile)
That, at least, is refreshing. If not me, who then would you like to discuss?

FRANK
Perhaps…the Führer, Herr Best.

BEST
The Führer himself? Of course.

He coughs to cover a laugh, then settles further into his chair.

BEST
Contrary to what you may think…I was never captivated by Adolf Hitler. I had my own ideas—ideals, if you will. I remember one time, there had been trouble with terrorists in Denmark. The Führer ordered me to make reprisals: counter-terrorism, as it were. Five to one. Five of them for every Nazi; then if that didn't work, ten to one. I did not follow his orders. I knew it would only create martyrs.
(a thin smile crosses his lips)
We did not need martyrs in Denmark. I was denounced and ordered to report to the Führer in Berchtesgaden. He behaved like a madman and when I left…
(he leans forward and lowers his voice)
…a conviction overtook me that our Führer was…mentally deranged.
(he nods his head, confirming what he just said)
His unchecked rage, his stereotyped repetition of meaningless arguments; his refusal to listen to anyone or anything, convinced me. The Führer had become what I thought of, at the time, as the *rasende*—the raving—Prophet.

FRAU BEST
(smiles, to Frank)
Your family owns a nursery. How nice.

Best silences his wife's interruption with a scowl.

BEST
Another time, the Führer ordered me to totally ignore the King of Denmark and the entire royal family. All because of a perceived—but undoubtedly correct—insult to him by the King.

>   (chuckles)
> The Führer had sent a long, flowery telegram to King Christian on his birthday. At long last, the King's acknowledgement arrived. A telegram with the single word, "*Tak*"—which means, "Thanks."

Frank laughs.

>   BEST
>   (stern)
> You think that's amusing, Herr Brandenburg?

Frank makes no apologies. It's a relief to laugh.

>   FRANK
> Yes.

Best chuckles with him.

>   BEST
> So do I. So do I. But not nearly as amusing as another story about the Führer and the Danish King.
>   (thoroughly enjoying himself)
> It was said the Führer sent the King a long dispatch in which he suggested the two Germanic sister countries of Germany and Denmark become one nation. Receiving no reply, he repeated his suggestion and, once again, awaited the King's answer. When no reply came, he fired off a telegram demanding an answer. He got it. King Christian is supposed to have wired back: "I have given your suggestion much thought. But at my age, I think I'm too old to rule over two countries."

Frank and Best both laugh.

DISSOLVE TO:

>   BEST
> Himmler was really a simple man. To him, one was either very good or very bad.

>   FRANK
> Was he religious? He couldn't have been.

>   BEST
> He apparently believed in God; at least he issued an edict that everyone in the SS must believe in God, although which God was never defined. It could have been Odin or Thor, I sup-

pose. What he, himself, actually believed was unclear, though he was something of a romantic mystic. Like Hitler he was superstitious and believed in such things as astrology, mesmerism, black magic. A curious role model, Reichsführer SS Heinrich Himmler: a man who let his life be influenced by soothsayers and charlatans…

137   EXT/INT. CAR (MOVING)—DAY

Frank is driving, map propped on the dashboard. This time, a POTTED PALM is strapped in beside him in the passenger seat. He is forced to BRAKE suddenly—and reaches over to steady the potted palm.

138   INT. GIESLER'S VILLA—DAY

Generalbaurat HERMANN GIESLER, 86, rises with difficulty to greet Frank. A short, wizened old man, bald with glasses riding high on his pate, a sallow, sunken face with small, rheumy eyes and a slit mouth; his scrawny neck seems too skinny for the collar of the white shirt and black tie that hang loosely on his slight frame under a black-checked jacked that seems at least two sizes too large.

SUPER: GENERALBAURAT HERMANN GIESLER

There is a cadaverous look about him as if Death has already staked him out. He extends a bony hand to Frank who takes it, surprised at the firmness of the old man's handshake.

139   CLOSE ON—GIESLER

> GIESLER
> Ah, yes. The camps.
> (shakes his head gently admonishing Frank)
> Do not let yourself be duped, my dear young man. The death camps, the crematoriums, were never built during the Third Reich. I would have known. Dachau is only a few kilometers from Munich, after all. There were labor camps. The ovens were built after the war. By the Americans.

> FRANK
> But—why?

> GIESLER
> To show that we—that the Germans—were bad. To justify their destruction of the Reich. No one was cremated. No one. Those ashes and splinters of bone that were found in the ovens—all fake!
> Fake! Analysis has shown they were not human at all. All those human cremation stories you have heard are propa-

ganda lies. Lies against the Third Reich and our vision of the future.

DISSOLVE TO:

GIESLER
Ah, the Reichsleiter. An astounding man, the Reichsleiter. I never saw anyone else work so tirelessly for the Führer and the Reich as Martin Bormann. I liked the man, Herr Brandenburg. I admired him.

FRANK
Did he die in Berlin, Herr Professor? Or did he survive?

Giesler sits in silence, his mouth working slowly. He lifts a skeletal hand and points a skin-and-bone finger at Frank.

GIESLER
Let us say, my dear young man, that I have no direct knowledge in this matter.
(his lips split into a thin smile)
Let us also say that as far as I'm concerned, Martin Bormann was the ultimate survivor.
(beat)
And let us say no more about it.

140   INT. JORDAN APARTMENT—DAY

FRAU JORDAN ushers Frank into a high-ceilinged room, simply and sparsely furnished. A balding man, RUDOLF JORDAN, 70s, rises laboriously from a straight chair at a table covered with a white tablecloth. Frail, he is clad in a black suit with an over-wide yellow tie with black polka dots.

SUPER: RUDOLF JORDAN

He stands, unsteadily, and nods a greeting to Frank. Frank notices his unextended hand is trembling. It is difficult for him to speak; his words are slurred.

JORDAN
What do you want with me? I never give interviews. To anyone. What do you want? I never give interviews.

FRAU JORDAN
(bitterness in her voice)
Please sit, Herr Brandenburg.

Frank takes a seat as she exits. Jordan lowers himself back into the chair.

JORDAN
What do you want here?

Frank squirms.

FRANK
General Baur suggested—

JORDAN
Ah, yes, Hans Baur. It is only because he is a good and old friend I agreed to see you. I never give interviews.

FRANK
So I understand.

He reaches into his briefcase and pulls out a blown-up photo he prepared for Jordan: Jordan with Himmler, Heydrich and Wolff. He hands the photo to him.

FRANK
I brought you a little gift. A vintage photograph. Of you, and Heinrich Himmler, Heydrich and Gen. Wolff. *Bitte schon*.

Jordan glances at it—and recoils, a frightened expression crossing his face as panic sets in.

JORDAN
Why? Why are you giving me this? That is not me! That is not me! Why would you give that to me? What do you want?

Frank hurriedly stuffs the photo back in his briefcase.

FRANK
I am very sorry, Herr Jordan. I—I must have made a mistake.

Jordan's eyes shift uneasily. He speaks defensively.

JORDAN
It had to come.

FRANK
What had to come?

JORDAN
The revolution. There was no choice for me other than to join it. The time was ripe for revolution. I was not wrong in joining it.

FRANK
You mean when Adolf Hitler came to power?

                    JORDAN
                 (nods, yes)
          The revolution. Do you know how to tell when the time is
          ripe for revolution?

Frank shakes his head, no.

                    FRANK
          How?

                    JORDAN
          When the top dogs no longer give a damn—and the under-
          dogs can't. That is when. And that is when Adolf Hitler took
          over.

141   EXT. WEST BERLIN—BRANDENBURG GATE—NIGHT

New Year's Eve. Frank stands with a group of BOYS—friends—looking up at the shrine to the music of Wagner. Berlin is festive, noisy and bright.

                    FRIEND #1
                 (motions them forward)
          Come on…

They pile into a car and drive through the crowded streets.

142   INT/EXT. BERLIN—CAR (MOVING)—CONTINUOUS

The boys are stuffed in. Frank drifts in and out of his own thoughts, trying to join in but preoccupied.

                    KEMPNER (V.O.)
          *And now, Frank…what are your plans? Back to your flowers?
          Back to your studies?*

AD LIB laughter and camaraderie among Frank's friends. One boy holds up a bottle of CHAMPAGNE.

                    FRIEND #2
          Happy New Year—

Other boys pull out bottles of champagne. AD LIB laughter all around. Frank looks out the window at the celebrating Berliners going by, lost in his own thoughts.

                    KEMPNER (V.O.)
                 (in Frank's mind)
          Bormann…Bormann.

KEMPNER (V.O.)
*I wish you would go back to your flowers. I wish you would—
stay away from those men.*

[DISSOLVE TO:]

143   EXT. WEST BERLIN—CHECKPOINT CHARLIE—NIGHT

Frank sits with his friends along the Berlin Wall drinking champagne out of the bottle, looking down into East Germany; East Berlin, the Iron Curtain—and beyond: a gray, colorless land without years, new or old.

As midnight approaches, the boys, now drunk, throw CONFETTI and sing SONGS, boldly waving at the East German GUARDS in the towers. The Guards stand at the ready, not waving back as the boys on the wall begin singing an old German folk song…

BOYS
*…es kappert die Mühle am rauschenden Bach…klip, klap—
klip, klap—klip, klap…*

[SUB-TITLE:] The mill is clattering on the rushing stream…

One of the boys pokes a pensive Frank.

FRIEND #1
Sing!
(laughs and continues, loud and off-key)
Es klappert die Mühle…

BOYS
…klip, klap—klip, klap—klip, klapp…

At the sound, Frank suddenly straightens and takes note, trying to remember what the sound reminds him of. Suddenly it comes to him.

FRANK (V.O.)
(in his mind)
Klap, klap…Klappert…Klapper!
(beat)
KLAPPER!

KLAPPER. The name Wolff mentioned. The one he wasn't "ready to see."

Everyone breaks into a CHEER. The New Year is here. Frank joins in enthusiastically, singing at the top of his voice.

ALL

…klip, klap! Klip, klap…klip, klap…

144   KEMPER'S OFFICE

KEMPER

Klapper? (He frowns) I have heard of him, but I know little about him.

FRANK

Do you think he could be—useful?

KEMPER

I think he might be—dangerous.

FRANK

Why?

KEMPER

He was in the SS—but nothing concrete is known about him. Always a bad sign.

FRANK

But—do you think he might have information? About Bormann?

KEMPER

Frank. You have come to me for guidance. I have given it to you. My advice to you now—forget about Klapper. Don't get in too deep. But—whatever you do—be careful. Be very careful…

145   DIFFERENT SHOT

Frank is leaving Kemper's office. He looks perturbed, uncertain.

146   STREET

Frank is walking away from Kemper's Office Building. He is in deep, concerned thought. Absentmindedly he steps off the sidewalk into the bicycle lane, causing a bicyclist almost to fall to avoid him.

BICYCLIST

Idiot! Look where you are going, you *throttle*! Make up your mind!

Frank gets a determined look on his face and walks rapidly on.

147   EXT. KARLSRUHE—SOPHIENSTRASSE—GUN STORE—DAY

Medard Klapper's GUN STORE. Frank stands before the display windows. The entrance is secured by a locked iron-bar door. Frank buzzes and the door clicks open.

A stout, casually clad, dark-haired man in his 60s, MEDARD KLAPPER, greets him with an out-stretched, over-sized hand.

SUPER: MEDARD KLAPPER

KLAPPER
Ach, ja. A pleasure to meet you. How can I be of help?

His casual air is belied by a nervous tension and eyes that dart suspiciously towards the street from time to time.

Frank reaches in his pocket, pulls out General Wolff's ring and shows it to Klapper whose eyes widen, then dart from ring to door and back again.

KLAPPER
The general's ring! How do you come to possess Generaloberst Karl Wolff's ring?

FRANK
The general gave it to me…to facilitate my studies.

Tentatively Klapper holds out his hand. Frank gives it to him. Reverently he holds it, then he starts to open it—

148   CLOSE SHOT—RING

It is being opened to show the little hidden compartment in the head.

KAPPER (V.O.)
The cyanide compartment.

149   WIDER ANGLE

KLAPPER
Thank God he did not have to use it…Like Goebbels, and—
(He lets the sentence die)

He gives the ring back to Frank. He pockets it. Klapper nods toward the door.

KLAPPER
It would be better if we didn't talk here. There is a coffee shop across the street. We can talk there. They have nice, secluded booths. For security—yours as well as mine.

150   EXT. KARLSRUHE—SOPHIENSTRASSE—CONTINUOUS

Frank and Klapper cross the street, Klapper's eyes flitting up and down—not only to check on traffic.

151   INT. COFFEE SHOP—DAY

Frank and Klapper sit at a booth in a window with a clear view of the gun shop across the street. Klapper turns his attention to Frank.

                    KLAPPER
          And he gave you the ring. *Donnerwetter!*
                    (peers at him, impressed)
          I never met him myself. Saw him, of course, many times.
          When I served in the Leibstandarte Adolf Hitler. A very
          important man…Of course, I was not important enough to
          meet him. But I know the general was often in the company
          of the Führer himself.
                    (his eyes flit to the window, then back to Frank)
          And I was told the general was fond of dogs. That he used to
          enjoy the Führer's three beautiful shepherd dogs. Blondie.
          And Wolf. And—and—

He looks at Frank, pretending he's trying to remember.

                    KLAPPER
          What *was* the name of the third dog?

                    FRANK
          The third dog?

Frank repeats blandly, unflinching. Klapper looks at him, eyes narrowing.

                    KLAPPER
          Yes. The third dog.

                    FRANK
                    (level-voiced)
          Muck.

Klapper's eyes crinkle in a smile.

                    KLAPPER
          Ja. Stimmt. Muck.
                    (settles back)
          Now. How can I be of help?

The Brandenburg Quest

This time the question is asked in a different way. He means it. Frank leans in.

> FRANK
> The general told me you are a man of much knowledge, Herr Klapper. He said you were a man of importance, of—of crucial involvement in both the—uh, old and the new.

Klapper seems to grow a couple of inches, then glances quickly at his shop.

> KLAPPER
> The general was too kind. What, specifically, do you want to know?

> FRANK
> I was told you might know something about certain…documents.

Klapper's eyes dart towards the window and he nods slowly.

> KLAPPER
> You are referring to the documents in Madrid.

Frank has never heard Madrid mentioned before but he responds quickly, not wanting to give away his outsider status.

> FRANK
> Yes.
> (beat)
> What can you tell me about them?

> KLAPPER
> It goes back to shortly after the war—

He stops in mid-sentence as Frank takes a small tape recorder from his pocket and places it on the table.

> FRANK
> Do you mind?

> KLAPPER
> If you want honest information from me, you must turn it off.

> FRANK
> Of course…

He turns it off and starts to put it in his pocket when Klapper stops him.

                    KLAPPER
On the table. Leave it on the table, where we can both see it. In the "off" position.
          (a beat while Frank obliges, then he continues)
As I was saying…it was shortly after the war. I was contacted by the Bormann group and ordered to arrange for the recovery of certain documents. About a dozen crates, I was told, were hidden in Dresden. In the Russian zone.

                    FRANK
What do you know about these documents?

                    KLAPPER
Only…they had been aboard a plane that crashed, then they were salvaged and hidden. The Bormann group told me they were of the utmost importance; that, under no circumstances, must they fall into Russian hands. Or any of the enemy allies. They must be recovered by us.

                    FRANK
And they were…recovered?

                    KLAPPER
They were.

                    FRANK
By you?

                    KLAPPER
          (shakes his head, no)
I was the agent only.

                    FRANK
What happened to them?

                    KLAPPER
They were sent to Madrid. To the Bormann group.

                    FRANK
Can you tell me about this group?

                    KLAPPER
They are still headquartered in Madrid. Today it is the Mariborsol, and—
          (stops, gives Frank a sharp look)
You *are* familiar with Mariborsol?

                    FRANK
                    (lies)
I have heard of it, but—
                    (the truth)
—no, I am not familiar with it, Herr Klapper. Neither General Wolff nor General Baur mentioned it to me.

                    KLAPPER
                    (nods sagely)
There was no reason for them to know. They were not among the…active.

His eyes dart to the gun store, then back to Frank.

                    KLAPPER
Such knowledge could be dangerous to possess. I presume you realize that?

                    FRANK
Nevertheless, Herr Klapper, it is necessary to my work that I know.

Klapper nods.

                    KLAPPER
The name is, of course, an acronym. *Mari* from Martin, *bor* from Bormann, and *sol*, the Spanish word for sun.
                    (smiles)
The rising sun of our cause. Mariborsol.

                    FRANK
And—the purpose?

                    KLAPPER
To ensure the future will be ours. Financial matters, for instance, and they are considerable—even on a world scale. Manufacturing. Real estate. All kinds of profitable investments and business ventures, controlled by our people, the people of Mariborsol, both old and new.
                    (smiles at Frank, a disconcerting smile)
Such as you, *nicht wahr*?

Frank smiles back, saying nothing, treating it as a rhetorical question. Satisfied, Klapper continues.

                              KLAPPER
And to guard the papers and documents handed down to us
from the Führer and the Third Reich—to guide us. Such as
the contents of the crates.
                                (beat)
The popular press has coined the phrase "The Fourth Reich."
We do not mind. It will be *our* Reich. The future will be ours.
Martin Bormann himself may not live to see the organization
that bears his name become triumphant, but triumphant it
will be!

Frank stares at him, poker-faced, and takes a deep breath. The Serail documents exist. Martin Bormann is alive…

                              KLAPPER
The Reichsleiter is convinced of it.

                              FRANK
Is, Herr Klapper.

                              KLAPPER
                             (nods, yes)
I myself had the honor of meeting the Reichsleiter. In Spain.
Less than four years ago. 1982. Of course he was an old man.
Eighty-two. But still as stocky as ever and remarkably robust.

                              FRANK
How did the Reichsleiter get out? Do you know?

Klapper shakes his head, no.

                              KLAPPER
But I know of someone who does? A former ODESSA man.
Are you interested?

                              FRANK
Of course.

                              KLAPPER
                              (sotto)
Lechner. Hans Lechner. He lives in Austria. I do not know
him. Only *of* him. But…if you show him General Wolff's
ring, he will give you what information he has.

The waitress stops by and refills their coffee cups. Klapper scribbles information about Lechner on a napkin and slips it to Frank.

The Brandenburg Quest

                              FRANK
     Thank you, I shall contact him.

                              KLAPPER
     You travel much, Herr Brandenburg?

                              FRANK
     Yes, my research requires it.

Klapper's eyes narrow, calculating the possibilities.

                              KLAPPER
     Then this is what must happen. In a few weeks I go to Madrid
     to meet certain Mariborsol representatives. You will go with
     me.

Frank manages to hide his alarm.

                              FRANK
     I?

                              KLAPPER
     Exactly. They must meet you. It will depend on what they
     think of you. Your future will depend on it: whether you will
     be accepted into one of the most vibrant and active groups
     working for our cause. It will be an honor for you. New vistas
     will be opened. As one of us, your work will gain new impor-
     tance…

Frank backpedals using his studies as an excuse.

                              FRANK
     But I am in school. How could I—

                              KLAPPER
                         (misunderstanding him)
     How? There is a strict procedure. For the safety of Maribor-
     sol—and your own safety. They meet us in a secret place.
     You'll be blindfolded. At a certain point…

Frank's head swims as Klapper's VOICE drones on…

                              KLAPPER (O.C.)
                         (bits and snatches)
     …body searches…code names…vows of secrecy…new
     BLOOD!

Klapper falls silent. Frank looks up. Klapper is eyeing him like a lizard on a rock. Frank stares back, unfazed, and continues as if nothing extraordinary has been said.

                      FRANK
     The neo-Nazi groups, here and abroad, Herr Klapper, are
     they a part of Mariborsol? Are they financed by it or are
     they—

Klapper's mouth stretches into a thin smile and he cuts him off.

                      KLAPPER
     Do not ask too many question, *mein junge*. Not just yet.
            (then he shrugs; another thin smile)
     Figure it out for yourself.
            (beat)
     And keep your trap shut!

Again his eyes flit to his store outside the window. This time he starts. Frank follows his gaze.

THROUGH THE WINDOW

TWO MEN are peering in through the iron bars of the entrance to the gun shop. Both are small, swarthy-looking; both wear wide-brimmed hats.

BACK TO SCENE

Klapper is visibly agitated.

                      KLAPPER
     There they are! I must go at once.
            (rises)
     You will wait here until we have gone into my shop. They
     must not connect us. They are not…important people.
            (he starts off, then turns back)
     You will decide about Madrid, then I will tell you…when.
     Meanwhile…there is a man I want you to see.

He pulls a pencil from his pocket, grabs a matchbook from the table and jots down a number, handing it to Frank.

                      KLAPPER
     Georg Stein. Ask him about his recent contact.

                      FRANK
     Contact? What contact?

                    KLAPPER
                    (hurriedly)
        Ask Stein. He will tell you.

                    FRANK
        But—

But KLAPPER is already half way out the door.

152   THROUGH THE WINDOW—FRANK'S POV

Klapper joins the two men, looks furtively up and down the street, then unlocks the door. They duck hurriedly into the gun shop—and close the door after them.

                                                          DISSOLVE TO:

153   INT. GEORG STEIN'S HOUSE—DAY

GEORG STEIN wears a white shirt and red cord trousers. Partly bald, long white hair hangs from the sides of his head around a moon-shaped face. A real-life Rumpelstiltskin.

SUPER: GEORG STEIN

A harelip causes him to lisp and, as he paces, his agitation makes his words harder and harder to understand.

                    STEIN
        I've never heard of this Medard Klapper. Why did he say he wanted you to meet me?

                    FRANK
        He asked me to ask you about—about your most recent contacts.

                    STEIN
                    (alarmed)
        Contacts? What contacts?

                    FRANK
        He said you'd tell me.

                    STEIN
        Contacts? About what?

                    FRANK
        I don't know. We had been discussing the documents on the missing tenth plane, and the Mariborsol organization, and he—

STEIN
(agitated)

Ach, du lieber Gott! Now I know why they sent you here! They think I know. They think I know something I should not know. But I don't. I don't!

FRANK

Know? What about?

STEIN

The Hitler documents.

FRANK

The ones in Madrid?

STEIN

Don't! Don't tell me anything!

He wrings his hands in agonizing thought.

STEIN

I feared this might happen. If they think I know, they—Oh, my God! They will do anything to safeguard their secret…But you see, I—I have uncovered some, some information. From a Soviet source. I am now certain your people know of this. That is why they sent you here. As a messenger An intermediary, if you will. With a—suggestion that I co-operate with them. Or a warning—
(he suddenly brightens)
Here is what you must do. You must return to Karlsruhe—to your Medard Klapper. Convey my willingness to meet with him. To combine our knowledge. Is that clear?

Frank scowls.

STEIN

But first—there is someone in Munich you must see. He will let you know how much you can tell this—this Klapper and his Mariborsol, before a meeting is arranged.

FRANK

Herr Stein, I am not—

STEIN
(ignoring him)
I have not his name. Only an address. I shall give it to you.

The Brandenburg Quest 125.

                    FRANK
Herr Stein, I am not a messenger, or an intermediary—in this
or in any other matter pertaining to Mariborsol. I am not one
of their—errand boys.

Stein contemplates him, an ironic smile on his deformed lips.

                    STEIN
You *are* one of them. Already you have been used. And now
you will carry my answer back to them. They will expect it.

                    FRANK
I am a researcher. I am not a participant!

                    STEIN
You—*refuse* to go?

                    FRANK
I do.

                    STEIN
Have care, Herr Brandenburg. It is a dangerous game you are
playing. Your—Bormann friends will not be pleased. There—
there are still men who will kill for their beliefs.
          (he looks searchingly at Frank)
You will not change your mind?

                    FRANK
No.

                    STEIN
Very well. I shall go to Munich myself. My contact there
will—inform your Mariborsol of the situation. With all its
ramifications.

154   EXT. FOREST ROAD—NIGHT

A small car comes driving along the road, as if the driver was looking for something. The beam of a strong flashlight occasionally shines through the window on the passenger side searching the woods.

155   INT. CAR

In the dashboard light we see that the driver is GEORG STEIN. He looks worried. With his flashlight he consults a map, and we see a piece of paper with the number 66.

156   WIDER ANGLE CAR—EXT

The car is slowly driving on with the flashlight illuminating the edge of the woods. It comes to narrow footpath. On a short pole hangs a wooden sign, askew. The beam of the flashlight catches it.

157   CU SIGN

It reads 66.

158   WIDER ANGLE

The car stops and STEIN gets out. Aided by his flashlight he makes his way to the footpath and starts down it. Shining the beam ahead he can make out a small, dilapidated wooden hut in front of him. STEIN walks up to the door, with his flashlight he bangs on it.

> STEIN
> (calling)
> *Holla im haus! Holla!*

There is no answer. STEIN bangs again—and suddenly the door slowly opens. STEIN peers into the dark.

> STEIN
> *Holla! Hier Georg Stein. Holla!*

There is still no answer. STEIN enters the hut.

159   INT. HUT NIGHT

Except for STEIN'S flashlight it is dark. STEIN takes a couple of steps into the hut. He lets his flashlight roam the place. It is empty, except for a few pieces of discarded furniture, among them a three-legged dressing table with a cracked mirror. When STEIN plays his beam on it, it is reflected back to him.

Suddenly TWO DARK FIGURES leap upon STEIN from each side of the door. Startled he drops the flashlight. It falls in such a way that its beam is reflected into the hut by the mirror. It is the only illumination of the violent action that takes place just inside the door. Silently the TWO FIGURES, clad in black and distinguished only as even darker forms in the gloom of the hut, jab sharp objects into the body of STEIN. He screams—a scream that turns into a hideous gargle as his throat fills with blood—and then sudden silence. When his body hits the floor it is with an audible thump.

160   EXT. FOREST CLEARING—DAY

With a shrill, cacophonous caw a flight of crows catapults from the branches of a dead tree in a black cloud. CAMERA pans down the tree. At the foot of it a shape lying on the ground can be seen. CAMERA SLOWLY ZOOMS in on the shape.

161   STEIN

It is GEORG STEIN. At the foot of the tree, among the withered leaves, he lies dead. He lies on his side with his face turned outward and is fully recognizable. He is naked, except for a pair of longjohns bunched around his ankles and heavy mountain boots on his feet.

162   CLOSER ANGLE STEIN'S BACK

Several stab wounds can be seen, with rivulets of dried blood running form them. In his upper back two table knives are still stuck in him. The handles seem familiar, it is the pattern we saw in a restaurant in Munich…

163   LS STEIN

SUPER: Some time later, George Stein was found, naked, in a forest near Munich, murdered, stabbed to death with table knives.

164   EXT. STOIZENDOR, AUSTRIA—COUNTRYSIDE—DAY

(IT IS LIKE THE OPENING SCENE)

Frank is driving his car. The road winds up and down—as if the Alps end only at the sky

165   EXT. FRANZ LECHNER'S COMPOUND—DAY

Frank drives up and parks his car. As soon as he starts to step out, TWO BIG BLACK DOGS come charging out from behind a woodpile in SNARLING fury.

Heart-pounding, he jumps back in the car and slams the door, watching, breathless, as the dogs claw and scratch at the car door.

Over and over again, the frenzied beasts hurl themselves in rage at the car, the furious barking obliterating all other sounds.

Frank's shaking hand touches the gear shift…then slowly he removes it. He's come too far to go back now.

CAMERA PANS & ZOOMS to Lechner's house.

CUT TO

166   CU GUN ON TABLE (as in opening scene) CAMERA PULLS BACK to a TWO SHOT—FRANK and LECHNER at table.

LECHNER
Now—*who* are you? How did you find me? Why are you here?

The questions are fired like bullets.

                    FRANK
                 (flustered)
I—I—
         (he pulls a photo out his pocket and shows it to Lechner)
    Do you—do you know this man?

167 INSERT PHOTO

It is a photo of Martin Bormann.

BACK TO SCENE

                    LECHNER
                 (cautiously)
    Where did you get that picture? What do you want from me?
                 (sharply)
    Who *are* you?

                    FRANK
    I—I—was told you were helpful to him. Many years ago. I—

                    LECHNER
    Who told you that? Why are you here? Where did you get
    that picture?

The questions slam into Frank.

                    FRANK
                 (blurts it out)
    From—from our family album.
                 (lying masterfully)
    I—I want to find out what happened to—to my uncle. I am
    the nephew of Martin Bormann.

Lechner stares at him for a moment. Frank desperately tries to read his thoughts. Nothing. Only silence.

                    LECHNER
                 (quiet, menacing)
    What is it you want? How did you get here? How did you find
    me?

His hand, beside the gun, twitches almost imperceptibly.

Frank rummages in his pocket for a moment—nothing. His heart stands still, then…he finds what he's looking for and brings it out—General Wolff's SS RING:

The Brandenburg Quest

                    FRANK
              (holding it out to Lechner)
    A friend of ours—of Uncle Martin. General Wolff…gave me
    this. He told me—

He breaks off and lets Lechner examine the ring.

                    LECHNER
    Karl Wolff…*Erstklassig*—first rate!

He pockets the gun and sits across from Frank, fixing his blue eyes on him and breaking into a slow smile.

                    LECHNER
    Now, *Poldi*, what do you want to know?

Frank draws a long sigh of relief.

                    FRANK
    I just want to know what happened to Uncle Martin.

                    LECHNER
    I last saw him in 1946. September.
              (motions to window)
    Out there the Swiss, Italian and Austrian borders come together—

                    FRANK
    The escape route.

                    LECHNER
    Ja. He came by bus. With a blonde woman who said her name was Rosi. She was about thirty. I recognized your uncle at once. He was knock-kneed, your uncle. *Ja*? He was exhausted, *Poldi*. He stayed with me fourteen days in Nauders. In *der Alten Mühle*, no. six.

                    FRANK
    The old mill.

                    LECHNER
    Ja. We talked about the old days. He smoked like a crematorium chimney…
              (laughs)
    Remember?
              (Frank nods)
    And he drank, and how! Like a camel about to cross the Sahara. I took them to a safe hut in the mountains, near the

border, then into Italy. To Reschen. Then by car to Brizen. He got his passport and a driver's license at the Papal Prefecture. They were sent to Genoa, then Istanbul…then Argentina.
>   (beat)
> There, *Poldi*. Are you satisfied?

                    FRANK
> You think he reached safety?

                    LECHNER
> Yes, of course. And I should know, shouldn't I? I, who personally took him across the border out of Germany.
>   (beat)
> And a blessing it was that he got away. It was a sign.
>   (Breaking off)

                    LECHNER (CONT)
> We will be back, Herr Brandenburg, we will be back—when the time is right. Your uncle and his organization have ensured that. It will not be us, the old cadre. Too late for that. But—with new blood. Men and women as devoted and loyal to the ideals of the Führer as we are.
>   (he looks sharply at Frank)
> New blood, Herr Brandenburg, new blood…

                    FRANK
> Why—why haven't you—eh—done anything by now?

                    LECHNER
> But we have, Poldi, but not in the—the limelight. We have been—we ARE preparing. For the day the time is right.
>   (fervently)
> I *know* my beloved Führer will be resurrected some day.

Frank stares at the man.

168   EXT. THE LECHNER COMPOUND—DAY

Frank's car comes driving out the compound. It stops on the road. Frank gets out. For a moment he stands staring at the distant mountain pass.

                    LECHNER (V.O.)
> I should know, shouldn't I? I, who personally took him across the border out of Germany…

FRANK fishes General Wolff's ring from his pocket. He contemplates it.

169 CU RING

In Frank's hand.

170 WIDER SHOT

Suddenly Franks hauls back and hurls the ring away into the shrubbery. CAMERA COMES IN to a CU of Frank, he looks content. CAMERA PANS OFF him to a shot of the MOUNTAIN PASS in the Alps, white and pure, serene and covered with snow, eternally fresh and bright.

END

SCRAWL
(Before End Titles)

Remains unearthed in Berlin in the 1970s were pronounced to be those of Martin Bormann, but many scholars and scientists dispute that claim. The fate of Martin Bormann remains a mystery.

Hitler's personal papers have never been found.

The use of the name of Hitler's third dog, *Muck*, as a password between exiled Nazis ceased after the publication of the book, QUEST.

Frank Brandenburg today lives in Hildesheim, Germany, where, with his father, Karl-Peter, he manages the Brandenburg Nursery.

All the main characters in the film are portrayals of actual people.

END CREDITS

Bear Manor Media

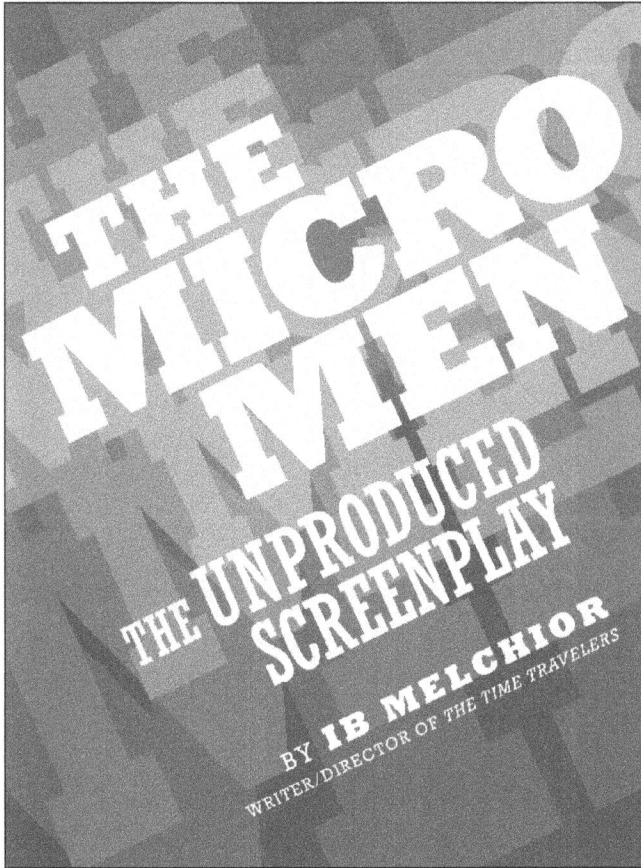

Classic Cinema.
Timeless TV.
Retro Radio.

WWW.BEARMANORMEDIA.COM

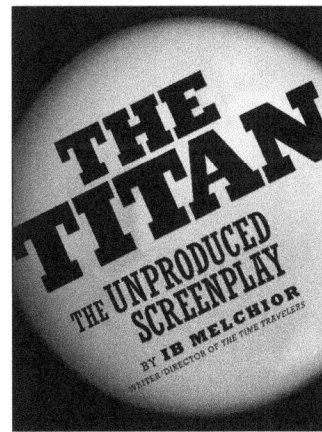

www.ingramcontent.com/pod-product-compliance
Lightning Source LLC
Chambersburg PA
CBHW080515110426
42742CB00017B/3118